Hoey & Co.
95-3308611
2615 MacFarlane Dr.
Lancaster, CA. 93536

IRONMAN'S

MASS-TRAINING
TACTICS

Size-Building Strategies For
Home- or Commercial-Gym Bodybuilders

by Steve Holman
Photography by Michael Neveux

IRONMAN's MASS-Training Tactics was written to help you reach your physical potential with sensible bodybuilding training strategies. Weight training, however, is a demanding activity, so it is highly recommended that you consult your physician and have a physical examination prior to beginning a weight-training program. Proceed with the suggested exercises and routines at your own risk.

ISBN 0-9627834-1-2
Library of Congress Catalog Card Number: 93-78362

Homebody Productions
P.O. Box 2800, Ventura, CA 93002

CONTENTS

ACKNOWLEDGEMENTS

The list of individuals involved in making this book a reality is almost endless, but I do want to mention a few people by name: John Balik, publisher of *IRONMAN* magazine and a true inspiration; Michael Neveux, co-owner of *IRONMAN* and master photographer; Ben Mall, who did a tremendous job with the cover design; Ruth Silverman, *IRONMAN* editor; Leon Bach, *IRONMAN* art director; Faith Walker; Bill McKnight; Tom Pearlman; Jerry Robinson; and Nadine Sondej.

Most of all I want to thank my family, including my loving wife, Becky; my daughter, Chelsea; my mother, Janice Pearlman; my sisters, Lisa Holman and Lori Paul; my father, Terry Holman; and my grandmothers, Cleo West and Carolyn Holman. Family is the backbone of success and accomplishment.

INTRODUCTION

If you're looking for that one magical mass-building routine, you can call off the search. Not because it doesn't exist—on the contrary, it does. In fact, as you'll soon realize, there isn't just one "magical" muscle-building strategy; there are several; and this book is a collection of the most productive ones. Ten of the best mass-building routines are outlined and explained in the following pages, each designed to provide the necessary ingredients for maximum muscle growth, along with that all-important twist of variety.

Every bodybuilder knows how important it is to vary his or her training. You need to give your body something different at regular intervals—for both physical and psychological reasons—if you want to pack on mass.

When you do the same exercises in the same combination for the same sets and reps at workout after workout, training plateaus are inevitable. You get stale, your gains grind to a halt, and great workouts become a fading memeory. On the other hand, when you change strategies, say, every six weeks, you crash through the barriers of size and strength at almost every session and fuel the fires of enthusiasm.

For those of you who train in a home gym and think that limits the number of exercises and techniques you can use, making it difficult, if not impossible, to alter your program often, this book will change your attitude. The routines are designed so that even if you only have access to basic equipment you can still take full advantage of every one of them.

Each strategy gives you that something extra to invigorate your effort and stimulate new gains. The 20-Rep Squat Routine.

Mass by Shawn Ray

The Rotation-for-Recuperation schedule. The Power Pyramid Program. Positions-of-Flexion Pre-ex. Target-Overload Training. These regimens, plus the others in this book, will give you the ammunition you need to alter your workout strategy every so often and keep your motivation and your mass gains on a constant upward trajectory.

The premise of this book is simple: Don't let your training routine become routine. Change is an ally in your battle to build muscle. Don't be afraid of it or ignore it. As I said in *IRONMAN*'s *Home Gym Handbook*, "We strive for order, but we thrive on change." Let's alter that quote to one that's more mass-oriented: "We strive for order, but we *grow* with change." All it takes is to do something different—just modify your method of attack by integrating one of the following 10 tactics, and you'll renew your enthusiasm and spur new muscle size above and beyond your wildest dreams.

PREFACE

Because this book is a sister publication to *IRONMAN's Home Gym Handbook*, it's only appropriate to begin with an overview of the first book. This will help you use more effectively not only the bodybuilding regimens outlined here, but also any routine you choose. The following are a few of the important points from *IRONMAN's Home Gym Handbook*:

•*Always use a phase-training approach.* "Phase training" means that you cycle your intensity; for example, you do four to six weeks of all-out training, during which you take every set other than warmups to at least positive failure, alternated with two weeks of lower-intensity workouts, during which you stop all sets one to two reps short of positive failure. This allows you to completely recover, avoid overtraining and build muscle much faster. (Phase training is based on Dr. Hans Selye's General Adaptation Syndrome model, which is explained in *IRONMAN's Home Gym Handbook.*)

•*Don't neglect your warmup set or sets.* Studies show that you can achieve 20 percent more muscle stimulation when you warm up properly.

•*Use intensity techniques sparingly.* When you incorporate forced reps, 1 1/4 reps, negatives, rest/pause and the other high-intensity methods described in *IRONMAN's Home Gym Handbook* into your routine, you up your effort considerably and are more vulnerable to overtraining. Never do more than 10 of these extended sets in any one workout.

Intensity by Lee Labrada

•*Rely on the big, basic exercises to develop mass.* Multi-joint movements, such as squats, presses, deadlifts, chins, dips and variations thereof should be at the core of any mass-building routine.

•*Work harder, not longer.* Don't ever add a lot of sets to your routine. In fact, you should never do more than 24 total sets in any one session, and most bodybuilders will make optimal gains with less. Remember, intensity, not duration, is the key to building muscle. Case in point: the distance runner's thighs, which are thin and stringy from an overabundance of low-intensity training, vs. those of a sprinter, which are thick and muscular from short workouts consisting of high-intensity bursts of effort.

•*Always use variation.* If you're bored with your workout, that indicates a need for something fresh to make it more interesting.

This book picks up that last point and gives you, the home- or commercial-gym bodybuilder, the details you need for productive change. Overhauling your routine every so often is one of the most effective boredom-blasting methods you can use, and this book is your blueprint for workout redesign. If you use these routines correctly and systematically, you'll build inordinate amounts of muscle in record time. Train hard, intelligently and efficiently—and good luck.

Chapter 1

ROTATION FOR RECUPERATION

In *IRONMAN's Home Gym Handbook* the point was made that if you want to build mass as rapidly as possible, you should make phase training, or intensity cycling, one of your basic bodybuilding tools. You've undoubtedly noticed the phase-training concept in the various periodization programs that turn up frequently in bodybuilding magazines, and you've probably heard quite a few people talking about its muscle-building benefits. Talking about it and actually doing it are two completely different things, however.

So many trainees swear by the phase approach—they just never quite get around to switching to those necessary low-intensity workouts that allow the body's recovery system to complete its job. Here's why:

•When gains are coming at a furious pace, you don't want to cut back your intensity for fear of slamming on the bodybuilding brakes.

•When you're making slow-to-no gains, you reason that the only way to get past the plateau is with gut-busting effort.

Because most bodybuilders spend their training careers in one or the other of these situations, they keep the pedal to the metal at almost every workout. Unfortunately, as you probably already know, if you push yourself constantly without a break, you can drive your body into an overtraining rut that's as deep as the Grand Canyon.

For all of those trainees who understand and believe in the phase-training concept—and let's hope that's the majority—but who never feel that the time is right to crank down the intensity, there is a way to shift into low gear without being fully conscious that you're doing it. You just employ a little psychological trickery, which can go a long way when you're trying to temper the obsession for mass that keeps you pushing to the limit every time you hit the iron. It's easy enough to do: Simply overhaul your exercises—and I mean every one—every four to six weeks. This is the Rotation-for-Recuperation concept, and it's a good one.

By completely revamping your routine, you can still go all out without really going all out. Although that may sound contradictory, it's not if you understand the concept of specificity of training and how your body adapts to high-intensity work. When you incorporate a new exercise into your workout, it usually takes a week or two for your body to get used to it. For the first three or four sessions your coordination improves, and you eventually find the right groove. In other words, during those initial workouts you learn how to efficiently perform the movement so that you contract the fibers in the working muscles or muscle groups more effectively.

You've no doubt noticed how fast your strength improves on a new exercise for the first few weeks. The learning process is part of the reason that this strength surge occurs. What you may not realize is that during those two weeks of learning—or relearning—an exercise, your intensity is lower, even if you're going to failure on the new movement. So you can see how changing your entire exercise lineup will automatically lower your intensity a notch or two for a few workouts.

Let's say that you want to follow proper phase-training protocol—four to six weeks of high-intensity training followed by two weeks of low-intensity work—but you just can't corral your motivation long enough to stop your sets short of positive failure. You have a couple of choices:

1) Do completely different routines every six weeks, pushing every set to positive failure, or at least very close to it. This automatically builds in two weeks of lower-intensity work as

you relearn the new exercises, which are followed by four weeks of higher-intensity sessions after your coordination and muscle-contracting abilities get up to speed.

2) Do your favorite routine for four to six weeks, then do a completely new workout for one week before going back to your original routine for another four to six weeks. Here you get a lower-intensity learning phase during the one week of new exercises as well as during the first week back on your old program.

Use this Rotation-for-Recuperation tactic throughout your bodybuilding career to help avoid overtraining and to spark more growth. It works with any training strategy. Take a look at the two basic routines at the end of this chapter and you'll get a true understanding of this concept. All of the routines in this book come with an alternate so that you can incorporate Rotation for Recuperation in whichever approach you choose.

Phase training is essential for fast rapid mass gains, so don't be afraid of a little psychological trickery. With it you can treat yourself to some monstrous size and strength.

Arm by Paul Jean-Guillaume

Following a high-intensity workout, up to 72 hours of rest (and in some cases more) is needed for growth to occur.

MIKE MENTZER
Heavy Duty

Basic Routine 1

Monday & Thursday

Quadriceps	Squats	2 x 10-15
Hamstrings	Stiff-legged deadlifts	1 x 10-15
Chest	Bench presses	2 x 8-12
Lats	Chinups	
	or	
	Pulldowns	2 x 8-12
Midback	Bent-over barbell rows	
	or	
	Cable rows	1 x 8-12
Deltoids	Behind-the-neck presses	2 x 8-12
	Wide-grip upright rows	1 x 8-12
Calves	One-legged calf raises	
	or	
	Standing calf machine	2 x 12-20
Triceps	Lying triceps extensions	1 x 8-12
Biceps	Barbell curls	1 x 8-12
Abdominals	Crunches	1 x 15-25

You need constant change in your training so that your body doesn't get used to the same routine.

SANDY RIDDELL
IRONMAN, **August '93**

Basic Routine 2

Monday & Thursday

Quadriceps	One-leg squats	
	or	
	front squats	2 x 10-15
Hamstrings	Leg curls	
	or	
	Good mornings	1 x 10-15
Chest	Incline dumbbell presses	2 x 8-12
Lats	Undergrip chins	
	or	
	Undergrip pulldowns	2 x 8-12
Midback	Incline dumbbell rows	
	or	
	T-bar rows	1 x 8-12
Deltoids	Seated dumbbell presses	2 x 8-12
	Lateral raises	1 x 8-12
Calves	Donkey calf raises	2 x 12-20
Triceps	Bench dips	1 x 8-12
Biceps	Alternate dumbbell curls	1 x 8-12
Abdominals	Reverse crunches	1 x 15-25

Chapter 2
ANABOLIC ACCELERATION

$\mathbf{T}$he squat is responsible for building more muscle than any other exercise in bodybuilding history. It's been used by almost every big name in the sport throughout the ages to pack on tremendous mass in the quickest time possible. The squat has been called everything from the natural anabolic to the exercise bodybuilders love to hate, and for good reason. It's tough, and it works. It's a difficult, feared, revered exercise—truly the king of the mass movements.

In his book *Super Squats*, Randall Strossen says the following about the 20-Rep Squat regimen:

Men who had been unable to register significant gains with other routines were suddenly gaining 20 pounds of muscle in a month or two.

Strossen himself claims to have gained 30 pounds of muscle in six weeks on such a program, and he's a relatively small-boned man.

The squat makes it almost simple to gain size. I say almost because this exercise is far from simple when you take a set to the outer limits. Perhaps the more correct way to put it is that it makes size more accessible.

Do your breathing-squat set only after you've started with two progressively heavier warmup sets. Here's how to perform this productive power exercise properly:

•Place a barbell bar on a squat rack and load it with a poundage that you can squat with in normal fashion for 12 reps, but tell yourself that you'll accept nothing less than 20.

•Take the loaded bar from the rack and place it at about the midtrap line across your back. (You might want to drape a towel across your upper back before shouldering the bar.) The bar will be pushing against your rear-delt heads and should feel somewhat low on your upper back but very stable. Your feet should be just beyond shoulder width apart, with your toes angled slightly outward.

•Take a couple of breaths, and then inhale as you begin your descent. Keep your back flat—no rounding—and your eyes focused straight ahead. Don't look up, or your lower back will arch, which can lead to aches and injuries. You also want to keep your torso as upright as possible. This descent should take two to three seconds.

•When the tops of your thighs dip just below parallel to the floor, explode, but don't bounce, out of the squat and ram the weight back up to the starting position as you exhale.

•Take three deep breaths and start your second descent as you inhale for the fourth time. You'll never take less than three deep breaths between reps, and after about your 10th rep you'll probably need six to 10 breaths to keep going.

•Do everything in your power to get 20 reps. Don't quit. Once you get to 20, rack the weight and move immediately to pullovers, breathing deep during each rep. Inhale on the way down, and exhale on the way up. This will stimulate your recovery and your metabolism as well as expand your rib cage.

•At your next workout and every workout thereafter up your squat poundage by five and get 20 reps again.

Pullovers, demonstrated here by Mike Quinn, are the perfect complement to breathing squats. This exercise stimulates recovery and has the ability to expand your rib cage.

From the above description it doesn't sound as if this technique is all that difficult. If you've ever done breathing squats, however, you know all too well that they're a masochistic trip through hell. Here's a telling paragraph from Stuart McRobert, author of *Brawn* and *IRONMAN*'s Hardgainer column, that drives home this point:

> *This exercise is beyond brutal. It takes a tremendous strength of will to keep doing rep after rep when your body starts to buckle. Your legs will be shaking, your back will be screaming, and your chest will be heaving up and down...but you will keep grinding out the reps [until you reach 20]. You may start having nightmares about having to do the same reps with even more poundage. Feed on this and make it into a positive thing.*

This brutality is exactly what makes the squat such an effective anabolic accelerator. When it comes to building mass, harder means better, which is why the compound, multi-joint movements outperform the isolation exercises every time when it comes to size stimulation—and the squat is one of the hardest compound movements around.

How many sets of this torture must you endure? Are you kidding? If you do more than one set, not only are you a glutton for punishment, but you'd better have paramedics standing by— 911 squats might be an appropriate name for this exercise. One set will be enough to stimulate plenty of new growth over your entire body—no matter how much bodybuilding experience you have. Remember that the squat works many muscle groups simultaneously, which is one reason why it's such an effective movement. When you squat hard and heavy, your thighs, hamstrings, glutes and lower back get the brunt of the work and your calves, abdominals and upper back get a secondary benefit—not to mention the effect on your respiratory and cardiovascular systems. You'll be huffing like a speeding locomotive after one 20-rep set of properly performed breathing squats.

Another benefit of the squat is its effect on testosterone production. Research shows that exercises that involve the large muscles, as the squat and deadlift do, stimulate the production of the growth-promoting hormones. You actually get a steroidlike anabolic effect from using these movements properly, which translates into intensely and infrequently.

"Intensely" simply means that you must push yourself to the limit—to momentary muscular failure. In other words you drive until you can't possibly do another rep, and then get two more. That's intensity. "Infrequently," on the other hand, may not be as clear. It means that you shouldn't abuse this exercise. Don't follow the more-is-better protocol that so many bodybuilders fall prey to. Squatting on two days a week will give you all the growth stimulation your body can handle without sending it into an overstressed, overtrained state.

The 20-Rep Squat Routine can work muscle-building magic on even the skinniest individual. Give it a try exactly as it's outlined—don't add exercises or training days—and you're guaranteed to get a massive growth spurt that will surprise even the hardest of the hardgainers.

20-Rep Squat Routine Tips

•Eat! Get plenty of nutritious calories but not so many that your abs do a disappearing act. Six smaller meals a day is better than three large ones.

•Do one to two light warmup sets for each exercise.

•Add poundage. Slap on an extra five pounds to your squat weight at every workout, but don't forget to add weight to your other exercises whenever possible as well.

•Don't overtrain. If you feel drained during the week, cut either the stiff-legged deadlifts from Routine 1 or the good mornings from Routine 2. You can also drop the two direct arm exercises at one workout as well, as your biceps and triceps get plenty of indirect stimulation from rows, chins and all types of presses.

•Don't use the 20-Rep Squat Routine for more than six weeks straight.

The squat is the best thigh-building exercise I know. At the same time it conditions the whole cardiovascular system.

ARNOLD SCHWARZENEGGER
The Education of a Bodybuilder

20-Rep Squat Routine 1

Monday & Thursday

Quadriceps	Squats	1 x 20
	immediately	
	followed by	
	Dumbbell pullovers	1 x 15-20
Rest five minutes		
Calves	Donkey calf raises	1 x 15-20
Hamstrings	Stiff-legged deadlifts	1 x 15
Chest	Bench presses	1 x 8-10
	Incline flyes	1 x 8-10
Midback	Bent-over rows	
	or	
	Cable rows	1 x 8-10
Lats	Chins	
	or	
	Pulldowns	1 x 8-10
Deltoids	Behind-the-neck presses	1 x 8-10
Triceps	Close-grip bench presses	1 x 8-10
Biceps	Barbell curls	1 x 8-10
Abdominals	Crunches	1 x 15-20

Squats resemble a magic wand of sorts...that's because, properly employed, their powers for rendering positive physical transformations are more awesome than anything else going.

RANDALL J. STROSSEN, PH.D.
Super Squats

20-Rep Squat Routine 2

Monday & Thursday

Quadriceps	Squats	1 x 20
	immediately followed by	
	Barbell pullovers	1 x 15-20
Rest five minutes		
Calves	One-leg calf raises	
	or	
	Standing calf machine	1 x 15-20
Hamstrings	Good mornings	1 x 15
Chest	Incline bench presses	1 x 8-10
	Flat-bench flyes	
	or	
	Pec deck flyes	1 x 8-10
Midback	Incline dumbbell rows	
	or	
	T-bar rows	1 x 8-10
Lats	Undergrip chins	
	or	
	Undergrip pulldowns	1 x 8-10
Deltoids	Dumbbell presses	1 x 8-10
Triceps	Dips	1 x 8-10
Biceps	Alternate dumbbell curls	1 x 8-10
Abdominals	Reverse crunches	1 x 15-20

Chapter 3

METABOLIC METAMORPHOSIS

T he deadlift is an amazing exercise. It has the capability to shift your entire metabolism into high-growth gear, which is the reason that it's often called the metabolic-metamorphosis movement. Although it's debatable whether the deadlift or the squat is the better size stimulator, one thing's for certain: The deadlift directly targets more muscle groups.

Not only does it work the lower back, thighs, hamstrings, glutes and, to a lesser degree, the abdominals and calves, just as the squat does, but it also hits the upper arms, forearms, shoulder structure and upper back—and not just indirectly, the way the squat does. This means that performing heavy deadlifts will make your entire physique—upper and lower bodies—thicker, giving it that powerful, awe-inspiring appearance. Your traps will start to grow, your thighs and hips will begin to ripple with raw power, and your spinal erectors will take on the look of two striated pythons crawling up your lower back.

The deadlift has actually been known to change a person's somatotype over a period of time—it can turn a skinny ecto-morph into a muscular near-mesomorph in a matter of months. The multiple-muscle training effect is why the movement is so incredibly productive—and also why it's somewhat dangerous.

Because the deadlift works so much of the body at one time, you must always exercise caution when incorporating it into your training. Not only can it cause an injury if you're careless with your form, but it can send your body into overtraining shock if you insist on doing too many other exercises along with it.

Here's how to properly perform the deadlift:

Deadlift by Bev Francis

•With a loaded barbell bar on the floor in front of you and your feet about shoulder width apart, squat down until your thighs are just below parallel to the ground.

•Grab the bar with a shoulder-width over-under grip—hands outside of your legs, one hand taking the bar with an overgrip, the other with a curl grip. This will help prevent the bar from rolling out of your hands.

•Keep your head up and your back flat.

•Take a deep breath and then stand erect as you exhale, driving up with your hips and legs as far as you can go. Your lower-back muscles should come more into play as the bar passes your knees.

•In the top position don't actually lean back, but pull your shoulders back out of the slump-shoulder posture.

•Lower the bar slowly back to the floor as you inhale.

•Take two to three deep breaths and repeat.

Be careful not to jerk on the bar. Pull smoothly, and don't bounce the plates off the floor. As you get stronger, you may want to strap your hands to the bar; however, it's best not to use straps until you absolutely have to so that your forearms are forced to bear their share of the work.

I remember when I started powerlifting and incorporated the deadlift into my routine after about three years of pure bodybuilding. Two months into my new power routine I went to the beach with a friend, and he couldn't believe the change in my physique. I'd added 10 pounds. "You look so much thicker!" he exclaimed. "What have you been taking?"

My answer was "Heavy deadlifts—twice a week."

You, too, will be absolutely amazed at the Herculean metamorphosis your physique will undergo once you start cranking out this get-huge exercise. The deadlift is truly in a mass-building class of its own.

I used [the deadlift] often when I trained with Franco Columbu. We deadlifted once or twice a week, never for more than three sets. The deadlift really gave our backs a massive look, and I think it accounted for the deep cuts and striations across our lower backs.

ARNOLD SCHWARZENEGGER
IRONMAN, **May '93**

Deadlift Routine 1

Monday & Thursday

Quadriceps, Glutes & Lower Back

	Deadlifts	2 x 8-10
	immediately followed by	
	Dumbbell pullovers	2 x 15
Calves	One-leg calf raises	
	or	
	Standing calf machine	1 x 15-20

Quadriceps & Hamstrings

	Alternate lunges	
	or	
	Leg presses	1 x 10-12
Chest	Incline barbell presses	1 x 8-10
	Flat-bench flyes	
	or	
	Pec deck flyes	1 x 8-10
	Feet-elevated pushups	
	or	
	Machine bench presses	1 x 8-10
Lats	Undergrip chins	
	or	
	Undergrip pulldowns	1 x 8-10
Midback	Bent-arm bent-over lateral raises	1 x 8-10
Deltoids	Alternate dumbbell presses	1 x 8-10
Triceps	Lying triceps extensions	1 x 8-10
Biceps	Incline dumbbell curls	1 x 8-10
Abdominals	Crunches	1 x 15-20

High-intensity exercise is not the only requirement for maximum muscular growth. Your muscles must be permitted to grow by keeping the total amount of exercise brief and infrequent.

ELLINGTON DARDEN, PH.D.
High-Intensity Bodybuilding

Deadlift Routine 2

Monday & Thursday

Quadriceps, Glutes & Lower Back

	Deadlifts	2 x 8-10
	immediately followed by	
	Barbell pullovers	2 x 15
Calves	Donkey calf raises	1 x 15-20
Quadriceps	One-leg squats	
	or	
	Smith machine squats	1 x 10-12
Chest	Incline dumbbell presses	1 x 8-10
	Decline flyes	
	or	
	Cable crossovers	1 x 8-10
	Bench presses	1 x 8-10
Midback	Bent-over dumbbell rows	1 x 8-10
Traps	Forward-lean shrugs	1 x 8-10
Deltoids	Military presses	1 x 8-10
Triceps	Bench dips	
	or	
	Close-grip bench presses	1 x 8-10
Biceps	Barbell curls	
	or	
	Alternate dumbbell curls	1 x 8-10
Abdominals	Reverse crunches	1 x 15-20

Chapter 4

SUPERSIZE SUPERSET STRATEGY

Supersetting, or alternating two exercises for antagonistic muscle groups, was a popular mass-building method back in Arnold's competitive heyday in the '70s. The Oak was notorious for supersetting chest and back exercises, a practice that would blow up his torso to immense proportions and have him strutting around the old Gold's Gym in Venice, California, like a peacock spreading its feathers. And with feathers like his who could blame him? Most of the big men used this technique to get even bigger during this illustrious era—competitors like Ken Waller, Franco Columbu and Mike Katz.

The legendary Bill Pearl was another bodybuilder who often used this technique, especially in his arm training. In fact, he wrote an article for *Muscular Development*, in which he proclaimed that supersetting biceps and triceps was one of his favorite methods for jarring his arms out of hibernation—and jar them it did. His arms reached a gigantic 20 inches, the sight of which caused more than one neophyte weight trainee to pursue bodybuilding with the obsession of a heroin junkie.

Arthur Jones, the creator of Nautilus machines, quantified the success that these and other physique athletes were having with this technique in the November '71 *Iron Man*:

> *Since working the triceps muscle also involves a far lighter form of work for the opposing muscle, the biceps, you can produce faster and better recovery by working your upper-arm muscles alternately—the slight amount of work provided for the biceps by working the triceps will cause the biceps to recover better than it would if it was rested entirely, and vice versa. Thus by working the triceps heavily during the rest period* between

Bench press by Brian Buchanan; bent-over row by Scott Wilson

heavy sets for the biceps, you will perform better during your second set for your biceps than you would if you did nothing between the two sets for your biceps. Far better results are produced by working faster—rest periods actually have an effect exactly opposite to that which might be expected in this case; instead of doing two sets for the biceps and then two sets for the triceps with rest periods between sets, do the sets alternately with no rest at all. Far better results will be produced in much less time.

Although Jones specifically targeted the biceps and triceps with his discussion, the question arose as to whether lifters might experience this productive training effect by working other opposing muscle groups with supersets. Arnold certainly found the technique to be just as result producing for chest and back.

So why aren't more of today's bodybuilders taking advantage of this tried-and-true approach? Good question. The answer lies in the way trends occur—in cycles. Although physique athletes back in the early '70s found supersetting to be highly effective and efficient, as with any other bodybuilding technique it had a few years of popularity and then became passé. Because variety is so important in the gym, even the most productive methods lose their luster and get shoved back into the closet after a while. What goes around comes around, however, and every few years daring bodybuilders hungry for new gains venture into that dark closet, dust off an effective, old technique, causing a resurgence. Considering the impressive results that Arnold and the others achieved, perhaps you'll want to start the superset ball rolling, and one of the best places to do that is in a home gym.

Using supersets is a much more realistic proposition for those bodybuilders who train at home than it is for those who train in crowded commercial gyms because there is less risk of inadvertent thievery. In a commercial gym there's always the danger that someone will take off with your dumbbells or the barbell you've set aside for your second exercise, and this can blow the superset, not to mention your entire workout. That doesn't mean it's impossible in a commercial gym. Just be sure you have a training partner who will watch the equipment for your second exercise like a hawk.

No matter where you employ this technique, however—at home or in a commercial gym—you must realize that it's difficult, especially when you superset two large muscle masses like chest and back or thighs and hamstrings. In this case you may run out of aerobic steam during your second exercise and cheat that bodypart out of growth stimulation. If you find this to be the case, keep your reps low on both movements—around six. Don't let yourself become so winded that you can't push your second muscle group to failure.

The superset routines outlined at the end of this chapter will produce rapid results. They are based on the big, mass-building basics. Here are a few suggestions to keep in mind when using this routine:

Tips for Supersetting

•Do a light warmup set for each movement before beginning your supersets.

•Go immediately from your first exercise in your superset to the second—taking no rest.

•Rest two to three minutes between supersets.

•Always keep your overall set total at around 20; supersetting is more intense than performing straight sets, so don't overdo it.

•Maintain strict form on all of your sets.

One of the reasons that the superset routine is so effective is psychological—when you superset two antagonistic muscle groups, you get an enormous pump in two areas at the same time and so you feel huge. Imagine your biceps and triceps simultaneously engorged to the bursting point, your arms looking more gigantic than ever before. Don't you think you'd feel invincible and get one heck of a mental boost? Try it and you'll probably end up doing the peacock strut, but don't worry. Arnold would encourage it. In fact, because you're using one of his favorite techniques, he'd probably demand it.

Arnold Schwarzenegger by Gene Mozee

Supersize Superset Routine

Monday & Thursday

Quadriceps & Hamstrings

	Squats or leg presses	1-2 x 6-8
	supersetted with	
	Leg curls	1-2 x 6-8
	Sissy squats	1-2 x 6-8
	supersetted with	
	Stiff-legged deadlifts	1-2 x 6-8
Chest & Midback	Bench presses	1-2 x 6-8
	supersetted with	
	Bent-over rows	
	or	
	Cable rows	1-2 x 6-8

Upper Chest & Lats

	Incline barbell presses	1-2 x 6-8
	supersetted with	
	Chins *or* pulldowns	1-2 x 6-8

Deltoids & Midback

	Dumbbell presses	1-2 x 6-8
	supersetted with	
	Behind-the-neck chins	
	or	
	Behind-the-neck pulldowns	1-2 x 6-8

Lateral Deltoids & Lats

	Lateral raises	1-2 x 6-8
	supersetted with	
	Pullovers	1-2 x 6-8
Triceps & Biceps	Barbell curls	1-2 x 6-8
	supersetted with	
	Lying triceps extensions	1-2 x 6-8

Abdominals & Calves*

	Crunches	1-2 x 20
	supersetted with	
	Donkey calf raises	
	or	
	Leg press calf raises	1-2 x 20

*Abdominals and calves aren't antagonistic muscle groups, but supersetting them keeps you in the superset mode and saves time.

[With superset training] I got incredible pumps. It was a fantastic feeling to experience a pump in the biceps and triceps or in the pecs and the lats at the same time.

ARNOLD SCHWARZENEGGER
The Education of a Bodybuilder

Supersize Superset Split Routine

Monday & Thursday

Quadriceps & Hamstrings

Front squats	
or	
Smith machine squats	1-2 x 6-8
supersetted with	
Leg curls	1-2 x 6-8
Leg extensions	1-2 x 6-8
supersetted with	
Good mornings	
or	
Hyperextensions	1-2 x 6-8

Triceps & Biceps Barbell concentration curls

or	
Spider curls	1-2 x 6-8
supersetted with	
Kickbacks	
or	
Pushdowns	1-2 x 6-8

*Abs & Calves** Reverse crunches · 1-2 x 20

supersetted with	
Standing calf raises	1-2 x 20

(continued on next page)

To stimulate increases in muscular strength and size, it is imperative that you regularly attempt the momentarily impossible.

MIKE MENTZER
Heavy Duty

Tuesday & Friday
Chest & Midback

Dips (elbows wide)	1-2 x 6-8
supersetted with	
Incline dumbbell rows	
or	
T-bar rows	1-2 x 6-8

Upper Chest & Lats

Incline dumbbell presses	1-2 x 6-8
supersetted with	
Undergrip chins	
or	
Undergrip pulldowns	1-2 x 6-8

Deltoids & Midback

Military presses	1-2 x 6-8
supersetted with	
Behind-the-neck chins	
or	
Behind-the-neck pulldowns	1-2 x 6-8

Lateral Deltoids & Lats

Wide-grip upright rows	1-2 x 6-8
supersetted with	
Pullovers	1-2 x 6-8

*Abdominals and calves aren't antagonistic muscle groups, but supersetting them keeps you in the superset mode and saves time.

Chapter 5

TARGET-OVERLOAD TRAINING

A training split that's becoming increasingly more popular in the advanced bodybuilding ranks is the Target-Overload regimen in which every bodypart is hit directly only once a week. Steve Brisbois, a former Mr. Universe and a successful IFBB pro, had the following to say in the October '92 *IRONMAN* after trying this unique mass-building approach:

Man, have I been growing. At first I was really sore, but almost immediately I noticed I became fuller, harder and I recuperated a lot faster.

The reason why this strategy is so effective is that not only does it allow each muscle group up to a week of recovery time before it gets bombarded with direct work again, but it also gives you a mental boost because you know that you only have to work one or two bodyparts each time you confront the iron. This concentrated focus gives you the mental and physical energy to really pour on the intensity and overload the target muscles.

Take a look at the workouts outlined at the end of this chapter, and you'll notice that this is an out-of-the-ordinary regimen compared to normal split routines. Here are a few things to consider when you use the Target-Overload Five-Day Split:

Tips for Target Overload

•Each session should contain about 12 total sets—15 is the absolute limit.

•The workout shouldn't take more than about 40 minutes to

Curl by Brian Buchanan

complete.

•Every bodypart should receive four to eight sets.

•Give each set other than warmups your all and go to at least positive failure on every work set. Feel free to incorporate intensity techniques like 1 1/4 reps, rest/pause and forced reps. These are very important because they allow you to blast the target muscle into oblivion without an enormous increase in volume, or sets. If you keep in mind that you're only training each bodypart directly once a week, you'll be able to maintain unusually high intensity and give each muscle group the blowtorch.

Here's how to split things up:

Monday: deltoids & calves

Tuesday: back & hamstrings

Wednesday: chest & traps

Thursday: quadriceps

Friday: arms & abs

Your goal is to go overboard on muscle overload and overtrain each bodypart to a degree. Because an entire seven days passes before each bodypart receives direct stimulation again, the muscle groups get ample time to recover from their slightly overtrained state, they adapt to the overload, and they grow.

Another thing that makes this routine so effective is the indirect effect. Bodyparts receive indirect stimulation even when you don't work them directly, because they act as stabilizers, which are muscles that hold your body in position so you can perform a movement, such as the way the abdominals assist during squats, or synergists, which are muscles that contribute directly to the movement, such as the way the triceps work during overhead presses.

For example, you work your delts directly on Monday, but they get indirect work from chest training on Wednesday and biceps training on Friday. This indirect stimulation helps facilitate recovery by removing waste products from the deltoids that were created by the direct-overload work on Monday.

Because of these size-and-strength-building benefits, the innovative Target-Overload Five-Day Split is worth using on a regular basis. By striving for target overload at one workout per week for each bodypart, you achieve plenty of target overcompensation and adaptation, which means that you hit the bull's-eye in the mass department.

[My training is] very high intensity. No more than 40 to 45 minutes with the weights. I do one bodypart a day every day.

FLAVIO BACCIANINI
IRONMAN, **September '93**

Target-Overload Five-Day Split 1

Monday: *Deltoids & Calves*

Military presses	3 x 8-10
Incline one-arm lateral raises	
or	
One-arm cable laterals	2 x 8-10
Wide-grip upright rows	2 x 8-10
Standing calf raises	4 x 12-20

Tuesday: *Back & Hamstrings*

Chins *or* pulldowns	3 x 8-10
Dumbbell pullovers	2 x 10-15
Undergrip bent-over barbell rows	
or	
Undergrip cable rows	1 x 8-10
Bent-over bent-arm laterals	2 x 8-10
Bent-over barbell rows	2 x 8-10
Stiff-legged deadlifts	3 x 10-12
Leg curls	2 x 8-10

Wednesday: *Chest & Traps*

Bench presses	3 x 8-10
Decline flyes *or* crossovers	2 x 8-10
Incline barbell presses	3 x 8-10
Close-grip upright rows	2 x 8-10

Thursday: *Quadriceps*

Squats	3 x 8-12
Sissy squats	2 x 8-12
Leg extensions	2 x 8-12

Friday: *Arms & Abdominals*

Barbell curls	2 x 8-10
Barbell concentration curls	2 x 8-10
Lying triceps extensions	2 x 8-10
Overhead extensions	2 x 8-10
Reverse crunches	2 x 12-20
Crunches	2 x 12-20

I believe in working out intensely, then allowing the body enough time for recovery....I train each bodypart once every five days.

DORIAN YATES
IRONMAN, **September '91**

Target-Overload Five-day Split 2

Monday: *Deltoids & Calves*

Behind-the-neck presses	3 x 8-10
Lateral raises	2 x 8-10
Dumbbell upright rows	2 x 8-10
Donkey calf raises	4 x 12-20

Tuesday: *Back & Hamstrings*

Undergrip chins or pulldowns	3 x 8-10
Barbell pullovers	2 x 10-15
Incline dumbbell rows	
or	
Bent-over dumbbell rows	2 x 8-10
Bent-over barbell rows	1 x 8-10
Good mornings	
or	
Hyperextensions	3 x 10-12
Leg curls	2 x 8-10

Wednesday: *Chest & Traps*

Bench presses	3 x 8-10
Flat-bench flyes *or* pec deck	2 x 8-10
Incline dumbbell presses	3 x 8-10
Forward-lean shrugs	2 x 8-10

Thursday: *Quadriceps*

Front squats *or* hack squats	3 x 8-12
Leg extensions	2 x 8-12
Sissy squats	2 x 8-12

Friday: *Arms & Abdominals*

Alternate dumbbell curls	2 x 8-10
Concentration curls	2 x 8-10
Bench dips	2 x 8-10
Kickbacks	2 x 8-10
Roman chair crunches	2 x 12-20
Reverse crunches	2 x 12-20

Chapter 6

THE POWER PYRAMID

M any bodybuilders tend to slack off their training in the winter months. With their physiques under wraps when the weather is frigid, they just don't have a lot of motivation to reach peak condition.

If you're highly motivated, however, you look at winter in a completely different light: It's the perfect time of year to pack your body with new raw muscle—mass that will shock your soon-to-be-envious peers when you finally peel off your sweats next summer and expose a physique that's denser than ever before. There's nothing like going to the beach on that first warm day and having people say, "Gee, you've gotten a lot bigger since last summer." Ah, the joys of bodybuilding.

You can get big at home or in a commercial gym, but for most trainees the home gym is the better place to launch your winter mass-building program for two reasons: 1) You'll never miss a workout due to the weather, and 2) you can set an environment that's conducive to peak performance for you—no coping with a gym that's so cold, you can't even get a pump. In a home-gym environment you're in complete, comfortable control, and control means that you have a better grip on manipulating and increasing your gains. Of course, commercial gyms also have their positives, such as the motivation factor, so train where you're the most comfortable.

What will it take for you to get more massive over the winter months? To build more muscle, you've got to do four things:

Stiff-legged deadlift by Samir Bannout

1) Slightly increase your food consumption.

2) Work out briefly yet intensely.

3) Don't miss workouts.

4) Add poundage to the big basic exercises at every opportunity.

Let's analyze this winter size-building plan of action to better understand the components.

During the winter months, when you're attempting to pack on extra mass, your physique is going to be covered from traps to calves most of the time. This means that you'll be able to eat a little extra food to feed your recovering muscles without worrying about definition-blurring adipose tissue, or fat. Remember that it doesn't take much of a food increase to build muscle. In fact, you can theoretically put on a pound of muscle a week with only 100 to 200 extra calories per day, so don't go overboard. This relatively small increase over the winter will allow you to build the maximum amount of muscle possible.

The extra calories will probably cause a small increase in your fat deposits as well, but don't let your fat phobia get the better of you. Keep in mind that this slight adipose buildup will be easy to lose when springtime rolls around and the weather invigorates you to start some type of outdoor aerobics activity. To ensure that things don't get out of hand, keep a close eye on your midsection. If your abdominals disappear completely and your lifting belt seems to be shrinking, it's time to trim your daily calorie intake.

One of the key elements to building mass in the winter months is motivation. Without it you tend to miss workouts, and when you miss workouts, your muscle gains begin to erode. Of course, staying motivated can be a real trick when it's 30 degrees and sleeting outside, so you need a program that isn't too long but still produces rapid, visible results—in other words, one that keeps you coming back for more.

The Power Pyramid Program fits the bill because you build maximum strength—and when you see your strength level increasing, your motivation will blaze like a forest fire. This type of program will help you achieve numbers 2, 3 and 4 of the requirements listed for mass building above—it consists of brief, intense, consistent progressive-resistance workouts.

The Power Pyramid Program is actually a modified strength-training regimen that's adapted from basic powerlifting training. You may have noticed that the powerlifting community includes some of the most massive athletes in the world—men whose size is merely a by-product, or side effect, of their quest for ultimate strength. One of the most effective techniques that these muscular athletes use to boost their strength levels is what is known as pyramiding. This involves simply adding poundage and dropping the reps on each set. For example, a powerlifting bench press workout might look like this:

Set 1: 135 x 12
Set 2: 185 x 10
Set 3: 225 x 8
Set 4: 315 x 6
Set 5: 350 x 4
Sets 6, 7 & 8: 380 x 1-2

To the average bodybuilder that may sound like quite a bit of work, but powerlifters can afford to do eight sets on the three powerlifts—the squat, deadlift and bench press—along with some assistance exercises because they don't have to cover all the major muscle groups the way bodybuilders, who are more concerned with developing their entire physiques proportionately, do.

Because bodybuilders use more exercises, they must modify the pyramid technique by reducing the number of sets per movement in order to avoid overtraining. If they did eight sets for each exercise, pyramiding the poundage along the way, their bodies recovery systems would soon shift into neutral, and the building process could jump into reverse, especially when they perform singles and doubles.

The power-bodybuilding pyramid is a five-set poundage progression, in which the first two sets act as warmups. Let's use the bench press again as an example. For power-bodybuilding purposes a bench press workout would look like this:

Set 1: warmup, 135 x 12
Set 2: warmup, 155 x 10
Set 3: 210 x 8
Set 4: 235 x 6
Set 5: 250 x 3-4

Obviously, the heavy pyramid is shorter here—only three work sets. After this big, compound movement you finish off your chest with an isolation exercise like dumbbell flyes.

Another good example is squats. Your squat poundages might go something like this:

Set 1: warmup, 135 x 12
Set 2: warmup, 185 x 10
Set 3: 285 x 8
Set 4: 300 x 6
Set 5: 325 x 3-4

Your thighs will be fatigued, but you'll still have sufficient glycogen reserves left to struggle through one hard, all-out set of sissy squats. This finishing isolation exercise will help you concentrate on the working muscles so you can squeeze the last bit of effort from the target bodypart. And because you're only doing one isolation set, you can really go all out. There's no holding back to conserve energy; treat this set like it's the last set of your life, and you'll get maximum growth stimulation.

One reason why this routine is so effective is that your set total always stays at 20 or less. With this work load you won't burn out, and you won't push your recovery ability to the breaking point. You'll stay motivated, be able to keep the intensity high at every session and grow bigger and stronger on your days off.

If you use the Power Pyramid Program religiously, you'll be

more massive than ever when summer rolls around. When you step onto the beach on that first warm day and nonchalantly spread your lats, people will think there's been a total eclipse of the sun. Now, that's big!

Power Pyramid Tips

•The workouts below do not include warmups sets. Do one to two warmup sets with 50 percent of your work weight on each exercise you pyramid. See the above bench press and squat examples. A warm muscle contracts more efficiently than a cold muscle, so if you're training in a chilly room, make sure you do two warmup sets.

•Whenever you can get 10 reps on the first work set of your power pyramid, up the weight on all three sets at your next workout.

•Go to at least positive failure on all of your sets other than warmups. If you start losing your enthusiasm try a moderate-intensity week—don't go to failure for four straight workouts. Then during the following week go back to all-out intensity

•Feel free to incorporate intensity techniques like 1 1/4 reps and forced reps into your training, but don't abuse them. If you start feeling overtrained, cut back on your use of these techniques. Intensity techniques will probably work best on the isolation exercises and/or the last set of a pyramid. (For a detailed description of the best intensity techniques and how to employ them for optimum results, see *IRONMAN's Home Gym Handbook*.)

•Take in extra calories, but don't get fat.

•Strive for strength and power, and size will follow.

What bodybuilders should be training to develop specifically is their strength. That's right. A properly conducted bodybuilding program is directed exclusively toward the development of strength. Why? Because muscular size and strength are related. It was discovered by scientists a long time ago that the strength of a muscle is directly proportional to its cross-sectional area.

MIKE MENTZER
Heavy Duty

Power Pyramid Program 1

Monday & Thursday

Quadriceps	Squats	3 x 8, 6, 3-4
	Sissy squats	1 x 8-12
Hamstrings	Stiff-legged deadlifts	3 x 15, 12, 9
	Leg curls	1 x 8-12
Calves	Donkey calf raises	2 x 12-20
	One-leg calf raises	1 x 12-20
Chest	Bench presses	3 x 8, 6, 3-4
	Incline flyes	1 x 8-12
Triceps	Lying triceps extensions	3 x 8, 6, 3-4

Tuesday & Friday

Back	Front chins	
	or	
	Pulldowns	3 x 8, 6, 3-4
	Barbell pullovers	1 x 8-12
	Bent-over barbell rows	3 x 8, 6, 3-4
	Bent-arm bent-over lateral raises	1 x 8-12
Deltoids	Military presses	3 x 8, 6, 3-4
	Lateral raises	1 x 8-12
Biceps	Barbell curls	3 x 8, 6, 3-4
Forearms & Brachialis		
	Reverse curls	2 x 8-12
Abdominals	Crunches	2 x 12-20
	Hanging kneeups	1 x max

*I swear by the instinctive [principle].
We're all different, and the only way
you find out what works is if you
experiment.*

SHAWN RAY
IRONMAN, April '91

Power Pyramid Program 2

Monday & Thursday

Quadriceps	Squats	3 x 8, 6, 3-4
	Leg extensions	1 x 8-12
Hamstrings	Good mornings	3 x 15, 12, 9
	Leg curls	1 x 8-12
Calves	Donkey calf raises	2 x 12-20
	One-leg calf raises	1 x 12-20
Chest	Incline bench presses	3 x 8, 6, 3-4
	Flat-bench flyes	1 x 8-12
Triceps	Dips	
	or	
	Close-grip bench presses	3 x 8, 6, 3-4

Tuesday & Friday

Back	Bent-over barbell rows	3 x 8, 6, 3-4
	Forward-lean barbell shrugs	1 x 8-12
	Undergrip chins	3 x 8, 6, 3-4
	Barbell pullovers	1 x 8-12
Deltoids	Behind-the-neck presses	3 x 8, 6, 3-4
	Wide-grip upright rows	1 x 8-12
Biceps	Alternate dumbbell curls	3 x 8, 6, 3-4
Forearms & Brachialis		
	Hammer curls	2 x 8-12
Abdominals	Incline reverse crunches	2 x 12-20

Chapter 7

THE HIGH-INTENSITY PRE-EX SPLIT

W hen it comes to high-intensity, pain-zone training, almost nothing beats the pre-exhaustion method. It's such a growth stimulator that Nautilus built the concept into many of its machines at great expense. You pre-exhaust a muscle simply by performing an isolation exercise immediately followed by a compound exercise for the same bodypart. This eliminates the "weak link" that exists in most multi-joint, or compound, movements.

For example, if you work your chest with the bench press, your smaller, weaker triceps will give out before you exhaust your larger pectoral muscles. In this case the triceps are the weak link. To get around this weak-link problem, you prefatigue the pecs with an isolation exercise, such as flat-bench flyes, before performing the compound movement. By doing this, you temporarily weaken the target muscle group and give the weak link a strength advantage in order to help push the target muscle to the limit. The same thing happens with biceps and back. Every time you do a pulling-type exercise for back, your biceps are involved. Because they're so important in the movement and so much smaller than the back muscles, the biceps fatigue faster, which means that you're not hitting your back muscles as directly as you could be.

Another example is triceps and deltoids, where triceps, again, are the weak link. Here's how to pre-exhaust your deltoids:

Grab a pair of dumbbells and crank out a set of lateral raises. Keep firing out reps until you can't get any more strict ones, approximately six to eight. This will thoroughly fatigue your side-delt heads. Immediately after you finish your set of laterals, take a loaded barbell—lighter than what you usually use on this

Leg extension and squat by Tom Platz

exercise—and push out a set of behind-the-neck presses. This will force your delt muscles to continue to work with the help of your stronger—for the moment—triceps.

When you do the behind-the-neck presses first, as is usually the case, your triceps give out before your stronger deltoids, and so your delts aren't really working to failure. In the above scenario, however, you pre-exhaust your deltoids with laterals, making them weaker, for the time being, than your triceps. While your delts are in this weakened state, you fire off a set of presses, which engage your now-stronger triceps and force your delts to work harder than ever.

Weak links are prevalent in almost all compound exercises. Here's a list of the major bodyparts, corresponding compound movements and the weak links involved:

Bodypart	Exercise	Weak Link
Quadriceps	Squats	Lower back
Hamstrings	Stiff-legged deadlifts	Lower back
Deltoids	Behind-the-neck presses	Triceps
Chest	Bench presses	Triceps
Lats	Chins	Biceps
Midback	Rows	Biceps

Although Robert Kennedy, publisher of *MuscleMag International*, is considered to be the creator of pre-exhaustion, it was Mike Mentzer who popularized this method and took it to the heights of its potential. While using it he won the Mr. Universe and successfully competed at the pro bodybuilding level for many years—and because this technique is so intense, his workouts were about one-third shorter than those of his competitors. He trained four days a week for 45 minutes to an hour.

Mentzer used pre-exhaustion throughout his bodybuilding career and made tremendous gains with very brief workouts. Once you try it and experience the pump and growth it produces, you'll see why it's considered one of the best strategies for upping your muscle mass.

Pre-exhaustion Tips

* Don't rest between the isolation movement and compound movement, or the pre-exhausted muscle will gain strength, rendering the technique inefficient, if not ineffective.

* Always keep the weight under control—no jerking or writhing around to get an extra rep.

* Never do more than two pre-exhaustion cycles for a particular bodypart; one is usually plenty. Remember that pre-ex is an intensity technique in itself—you're working harder, so do less for best results.

* Try to keep your direct arm work to a minimum—one set per exercise—or do only one direct arm workout per week to avoid overtraining your biceps and triceps. Your arms will get plenty of indirect stimulation from rows, chins and presses.

* Don't use pre-exhaustion for more than six weeks at a time.

Note: This discussion is not to suggest that pre-exhaustion is the only way to train. It's not. It's simply one of the many productive mass-building methods available to you. Use it, but don't get stuck on it. Doing compound exercises without a preliminary pre-exhaustion isolation movement is also very effective, as you already know if you've tried any of the routines in the previous chapters.

I would superset leg extensions with leg presses, going to complete failure on each portion of the [cycle] and getting plenty of forced reps in there in order to drive the muscle beyond muscular failure....I gained two inches on my thighs the first year.

LEE LABRADA
IRONMAN, **September '91**

High-Intensity Pre-ex Split 1

Monday & Thursday

Quadriceps	Leg extensions *cycled with* Squats	1-2 x 6-9
Hamstrings	Leg curls *cycled with* Stiff-legged deadlifts	1-2 x 6-9
Calves	Donkey calf raises	2 x 12-20
Chest	Dumbbell flyes *or* pec deck flyes *cycled with* Low-incline barbell presses	1-2 x 6-9
Triceps*	Dumbbell kickbacks *cycled with* Dips	1 x 6-9

Tuesday & Friday

Lats	Barbell pullovers *or* pullover machine *cycled with* Undergrip chins *or* pulldowns	1-2 x 6-9

Midback	Forward-lean shrugs
	   cycled with
	Bent-over barbell rows
	   or
	Cable rows
		1-2 x 6-9
		
		1-2 x 6-9

Deltoids	Dumbbell lateral raises *cycled with* Behind-the-neck presses	1-2 x 6-9 1-2 x 6-9
Biceps*	Barbell curls *cycled with* Undergrip bent-over rows	1 x 6-9 1 x 6-9
Abdominals	Crunches *or* machine crunches *cycled with* Hanging kneeups	1-2 x max

* The biceps and triceps aren't hampered by weak links, but by pre-exhausting them with an isolation exercise you can force them to work harder on a compound movement with the help of a stronger bodypart. In this routine the back pushes the biceps during undergrip bent-over rows and the chest helps the triceps during dips.

High-intensity training and a large amount of training are mutually exclusive factors. You can have one or the other, but not both. If you double the intensity of training, then you must reduce the amount of training by more than 80 percent to compensate.

ELLINGTON DARDEN, PH.D.
High-Intensity Bodybuilding

High-Intensity Pre-ex Split 2

Monday & Thursday

Quadriceps	Sissy squats	
	cycled with	
	Front squats or hack squats	1-2 x 6-9
Hamstrings	Leg curls	
	cycled with	
	Good mornings	
	or	
	Hyperextensions	1-2 x 6-9
Calves	One-leg calf raises	2 x 12-20
Chest	Incline dumbbell flyes	
	cycled with	
	Bench presses	1-2 x 6-9
Triceps*	Lying triceps extensions	1 x 6-9
	cycled with	
	Close-grip bench presses	1 x 6-9

Tuesday & Friday

Lats	Dumbbell pullovers	
	cycled with	
	Front chins *or* pulldowns	1-2 x 6-9
Midback	Bent-arm bent-over lateral raises	1-2 x 6-9
	cycled with	
	Bent-over rows	1-2 x 6-9
Deltoids	Seated dumbbell lateral raises	1-2 x 6-9
	cycled with	
	Military presses	1-2 x 6-9
Biceps*	Barbell curls 1 x 6-9	
	cycled with	
	Undergrip chins *or* pulldowns	1 x 6-9
Abdominals	Crunches	
	cycled with	
	Reverse crunches	1-2 x max

* The biceps and triceps aren't hampered by weak links, but by pre-exhausting them with an isolation exercise you can force them to work harder on a compound movement with the help of a stronger bodypart. In this routine the back pushes the biceps during undergrip chins and the chest helps the triceps during close-grip bench presses.

Chapter 8

POF: EFFICIENT MULTI-ANGULAR MASS TRAINING

Multi-angular training—using a variety of exercises to hit a muscle from more than one position—is a definite prerequisite for advanced muscle growth; however, to use multi-angular training correctly you don't simply pick a bunch of exercises for each bodypart and randomly shuffle them into your routine as many bodybuilders mistakenly do. Correct multi-angular training takes logical thought, a quality most advanced routines don't reflect.

If you analyze almost any advanced bodybuilder's routine, you'll find abuse of the multi-angular-training concept. Most bodybuilders just don't realize that for each muscle or muscle group there are three, and only three, positions that must be worked for full, complete development—midrange, stretch and contracted. Here's a general explanation of each:

•*Midrange.* You usually train this position with a multiple-joint, or compound, movement that works the muscle without total peak contraction or stretch—in other words, through more of a middle range. Examples include squats for the quads, presses for the delts and bench presses for the pecs. Most midrange exercises work the target muscle group with the assistance of secondary muscles that provide a synergistic effect. For example, squats work your quads, the target muscle group, with the help of your glutes and lower back. Because Mother Nature designed the human muscular system to function in this manner—with the muscles working as a team—this synergistic effect stimulates the bulk of the target muscle group as well as sufficiently warming up the muscle for the more concentrated work that hits the next two positions.

•**Stretch.** In this position the target muscle reaches complete extension, where the fibers and fascia, or fiber encasements, are in an extreme elongated state. This takes advantage of the prestretch phenomenon, or myotatic reflex, an action that can allow you to involve more muscle fibers and produce a more powerful contraction. A good example of prestretch is a baseball player swinging a bat; just before he swings, he quickly forces the bat back to prestretch the involved muscles. This gives him more power in his swing. With a quick twitch, not a bounce, at the point of stretch, you can get this same effect with stretch-position bodybuilding movements, which include flyes for the chest, pullovers for the latissimus, sissy squats for the quads and overhead extensions for the triceps. Note that at the bottom of these exercises you feel an uncomfortable pull on the target muscles.

•**Contracted.** In this position the target muscle is placed in its ultimate peak-contracted, or flexed, state with opposing resistance. Because of this peak resistance you get an intense contraction in the target muscle, but in order for this to happen in the most beneficial manner possible it must be completely and thoroughly warmed up, which is why you usually work this position last. In other words, you usually use contracted-position exercises to finish off a muscle for best results. Examples of contracted-position movements include leg extensions for the quads, kickbacks for the triceps, concentration curls for the biceps and leg curls for the hamstrings. Notice that there is resistance in the flexed position of each of these exercises.

This three-position approach is the basic premise of a logical, multi-angular strategy known as Positions-of-Flexion (POF) training. POF is an efficient training regimen that maximizes recovery and growth because it reflects the fact that you can work each muscle group completely with a maximum of three exercises. For example, a POF thigh routine would consist of squats (midrange), sissy squats (stretch) and leg extensions (contracted). Each bodypart requires a similar three-exercise attack that hits the three positions—and *that's all the muscle needs for total development.*

Most bodybuilders don't bother to dissect muscle function in this manner, and so their routines lack efficiency. They incorporate countless movements for each bodypart to "hit all the angles," using more of a shotgun approach. This usually means extensive overlap—many of the same positions are worked over and over in the different bodypart routines—which causes waste, which in turn causes unnecessary drain on the recovery system and leads to delays in muscle gains.

For example, an advanced deltoid routine might include the military press and the seated dumbbell press, among other shoulder movements. Both of these presses work the shoulders in a similar manner; that is, from the same midrange position, or angle. A thigh routine might include squats and leg presses, as well as other quad movements. Once again these are two very similar exercises in terms of training angles, and it is unnecessary duplication.

On the following pages is a listing of the three positions of flexion for each bodypart to help you further understand the POF concept:

Calves

Midrange: Toes-pointed leg curls work the midrange position of the calves. Hamstrings are the synergist muscles that help the calves move the resistance.

Stretch: You achieve total stretch at the bottom of a donkey calf raise—calves stretched off of a high block, toes pointed slightly inward, knees locked and torso at a right angle to the legs.

Contracted: You reach the completely contracted position at the top of a standing calf raise—up on toes, torso and legs on the same plane and toes pointed slightly outward.

Quadriceps

Midrange: Squatting- or leg-pressing-type movements work the quads' midrange position. Glutes are the synergist muscles that help the quads move the resistance.

Stretch: You achieve total stretch at the bottom of a sissy squat—torso and thighs on the same plane, with calves almost flush against hamstrings.

Contracted: You reach the completely contracted position at the top of a leg extension—torso and thighs at a right angle, lower legs extended and knees locked.

Hamstrings

Midrange: The top one-third of a barbell squat or stiff-legged deadlift trains the midrange position of the hamstrings. The lower back and glutes are the synergist muscle groups that help the hams move the resistance.

Stretch: You reach total stretch at the bottom of a stiff-legged deadlift.

Contracted: The top of a leg curl—torso and thighs on the same plane, with calves flush against hamstrings and feet flexed toward the shins—completely contracts the hamstrings.

Pectoralis minor *(upper chest)*

Midrange: Any incline-pressing movement works the upper pecs' midrange position. The triceps act as synergists.

Stretch: You reach total stretch at the bottom of an incline-flye motion.

Contracted: To completely contract your upper pecs you extend your arms and cross them over your upper chest.

Pectoralis major *(lower chest)*

Midrange: Any flat- or decline-pressing movement works the lower pecs' midrange position. The triceps act as synergists to help the pecs move the resistance.

Stretch: You reach total stretch at the bottom of a decline-flye motion—elbows back behind the torso.

Contracted: You completely contract your lower pecs when your arms are extended and crossed over your abdomen.

Latissimus dorsi

Midrange: Front-chin or front-pulldown movements—where your upper arms come into your body more from the sides than the front—work the lats' midrange position. The midback and biceps act as synergists to help the lats move the resistance.

Stretch: You reach total stretch at the bottom of a pullover movement—upper arms overhead with the elbows slightly below the plane of the torso.

Contracted: You achieve complete contraction at the bottom of an undergrip chin, undergrip pulldown, undergrip bent-over row or stiff-arm pulldown—upper arms down, close to and behind your torso.

Midback *(trapezius)*

Midrange: Behind-the-neck chins or behind-the-neck pulldowns work the midrange position of the midback. The lats and biceps are the synergists that help the midback move the resistance.

Stretch: You reach total stretch at the bottom of a cable row or bent-over row—torso upright but bent at slightly less than 90 degrees to the thighs, and arms extended with your scapulae, or shoulder blades, spread.

Contracted: You achieve total contraction when your scapulae are squeezed together with the resistance pulling on a plane that's almost perpendicular to your torso. For example, you reach this position at the top of a shoulder-width cable row, bent-over row, bent-arm bent-over lateral raise or shrug.

Upper trapezius

Midrange: You work this position during delt work with upright rows or lateral raises.

Stretch: You reach total stretch at the bottom of a forward-lean shrug.

Contracted: You achieve total contraction at the top of a forward-lean shrug with your shoulders pulled up and back as high as possible.

Deltoids

Midrange: Overhead pressing movements work the delts' midrange position. The triceps are the synergist muscles that help the deltoids.

Stretch: You achieve total stretch at the bottom of a one-arm incline lateral raise or a one-arm cable lateral—arm across the front of the torso.

Contracted: You reach the completely contracted position at the top of an upright row or lateral raise—upper arm out to the side and angled slightly upward.

Triceps

Midrange: Your arm is perpendicular to your torso, as in the bench press. Lying triceps movements work this position effectively. The pecs and/or lats act as synergists on these movements.

Stretch: Your upper arm is next to the side of your head, and the lower arm is bent back behind it, knuckles almost touching your shoulder, as in the bottom position of a standing triceps extension.

Contracted: Your arm is down next to your side, straight (elbows locked) and slightly back behind your body (the muscle is fully flexed). You work this position with triceps kickbacks or one-arm pushdowns.

Biceps

Midrange: Your upper arm is slightly in front of your torso, as in standing barbell curls or preacher curls. The front-deltoid heads are the synergist muscles that help the biceps move the resistance.

Stretch: Your upper arm is straight down and back behind the plane of your torso, as in the bottom of an incline dumbbell curl.

Contracted: Your upper arm is next to your head, your forearm flush against the upper arm, your palm down and your little finger twisting outward. This position is hard to simulate with any conventional barbell exercise, but nonsupport concentration curls will get you as close as possible.

Forearms *(flexors: underside)*

Midrange: You work this position with the gripping that you do and the movement that occurs when you perform other exercises, specifically any type of curl.

Stretch: You achieve total stretch in the bottom position of a wrist curl when your forearms are resting on a bench that's angled slightly upward and the angle at your elbows is more than 90 degrees.

Contracted: You reach complete contraction at the top of a wrist curl when your forearms are resting on a bench that's angled slightly downward and the angle at your elbows is less than 90 degrees.

Forearms *(extensors: top of forearm)*

Midrange: Reverse curls work the extensors' midrange position. The biceps and brachialis muscles act as synergists.

Stretch: You achieve total stretch at the bottom of a reverse wrist curl when your forearms are resting on a bench that's angled slightly upward and the angle at your elbows is more than 90 degrees.

Contracted: You reach complete contraction at the top of a reverse wrist curl when your forearms are resting on a bench that's angled slightly downward and the angle at your elbows is less than 90 degrees.

Rectus abdominus *(as a whole)*

Midrange: The midrange movement for the rectus abdominus involves the hip flexors to a degree. Remember, you're not trying to isolate the target muscle with the midrange movement, as a midrange exercise is usually a compound movement that allows surrounding muscles to help the target muscle contract. In this case the hip flexors are the helping muscles. You work the rectus abdominus through its midrange position with reverse crunches or hanging kneeups.

Stretch: The entire rectus abdominus is in the stretch position when the knees are bent at 90 degrees, your thighs are parallel to the floor and your torso is slightly below parallel to the floor, as in the bottom position of a Roman chair crunch.

Lower rectus abdominus

Contracted: You achieve this position when your upper thighs are almost flush against your abdomen and your hips are rolled upward, as in the finish position of a reverse crunch or hanging kneeup. (Note that the reverse crunch and hanging kneeup work the entire rectus abdominus through its midrange position and the lower rectus in its contracted position.)

Upper rectus abdominus

Contracted: You achieve this position when your upper torso is curled forward toward your pelvis while your hips and lower back remain on the same plane, as in the standard crunch.

Once you train a muscle in one of its positions, there's no need to hit that position again with a similar movement. This type of overlap makes workouts inefficient, and lack of efficiency is one reason why so many advanced bodybuilders work out for two to four hours a day, six days a week and are lucky to gain three pounds of muscle a year. They simply haven't taken the time to analyze the actual functions of the muscles they're working. If they did, their time spent in the gym would decrease dramatically, and their muscle mass would increase.

Unfortunately, misinformation continues to flourish as the shotgun approach is perpetuated from generation to generation. If one average bodybuilder sees or hears of a better bodybuilder doing something, he or she often adopts the practice without even thinking about it. It's totally illogical to adopt a technique or practice without putting it through a rigorous thought process; however, this lack of logic is one of the reasons that so many fallacies are hailed as gospel in the realm of weight training. Lack of rational thought is also the reason why it takes bodybuilders so long to reach their genetic potentials. Many will use techniques and methods that are nonproductive and sometimes downright detrimental for years and often decades because some Mr. Something-or-other was seen using it once upon a time.

As far as advanced multi-angular training is concerned, the time has come to change the current illogical practices. If you're in the late-intermediate to advanced stages of your bodybuilding career, try one of the POF routines given in this chapter. You'll be pleasantly surprised, if not shocked, as your muscle mass surges to new levels. (For a more complete bodypart-by-bodypart analysis of POF training, as well as other POF routine variations, questions and answers and exercise tips see *IRONMAN's Critical Mass—The Positions-of-Flexion Approach to Explosive Muscle Growth.*)

Mass by Lee Labrada

POF Training Tips

1) The standard order for the three positions is midrange, stretch and contracted. The midrange-position movement works the bulk of the target muscle with the help of synergist, or helping, muscles and warms up the target area for the more concentrated work to come in the next two positions. After the midrange exercise comes the stretch position, where you take advantage of the prestretch phenomenon. With a slight twitch at the bottom of any stretch-position exercise you can involve more muscle fibers and cause a more powerful contraction in the target muscle. Last is the contracted position, where the target muscle is flexed with opposing resistance—in other words, resistance doesn't fall off at the top of the movement. These exercises give the target muscle an intense peak contraction after you've sufficiently warmed it up and worked it in the other two positions.

2) Do at least one light warmup set with 50 percent of your work weight for every midrange movement.

3) Fight the urge to add sets. Two sets is plenty of work for any position, or angle. A good rule of thumb is to never do more than 25 sets at any one workout—and less is preferable. If an exercise has only one set listed after it and you want to do two, go ahead, but subtract a set from another exercise to keep your set total under 25. For example, if you want to do two sets for leg extensions in Workout 1, you could either cut your sissy squat sets to one or cut a set of an exercise for one of your stronger bodyparts. Many people don't feel that this is necessary, believing that advanced bodybuilders need more sets to keep making gains, but this is a fallacy. Advanced bodybuilders' nervous systems are much more developed due to their many years of training. This means that they can more readily contract more muscle fibers at any one time. In effect, advanced bodybuilders can train more efficiently simply

because of the neuromuscular development they have already attained. Advanced bodybuilders don't really need volume increases compared to the intermediate work load, only more intensity—they must train harder, not longer.

4) Keep your form strict—two seconds up and two seconds down.

5) The every-other-day split routine has you train half of your body on one day, rest the following day, train the other half of your body on the next day and so on. This facilitates recovery, but it also means that some weeks you train on Sunday and some weeks you train on Saturday. Those who don't like to train on the weekends can use the standard four-day split: half on Monday and Thursday and the other half Tuesday and Friday. This isn't quite as recovery-oriented as the every-other-day split, but it's still quite effective.

6) Always use a phase-training approach: four to six weeks of taking all sets other than warmups to at least positive failure, followed by two weeks of lower-intensity work, in which you stop all sets two reps short of failure. (See *IRONMAN's Home Gym Handbook* for a complete discussion of phase training.)

7) The POF Every-Other-Day Split 2 contains forearm work. Only include the forearm routine if this is a weak bodypart for you. Remember that your forearms will get plenty of work from the gripping and hanging that you do throughout the routine.

8) The POF Every-Other-Day Split 1 contains upper-trap exercise. Most bodybuilders get plenty of upper-trap stimulation from delt and back training, so do shrugs only if you need work in this area.

Many bodybuilders sell themselves short. Erroneously attributing their lack of satisfactory progress to a poverty of the requisite genetic traits, instead of to their irrational training and dietary practices, they give up training. Don't make the same mistake.

MIKE MENTZER
Heavy Duty

POF Every-Other-Day Split 1

Workout 1

Quadriceps

Midrange:	Squats	2 x 8-12
Stretch:	Sissy squats	2 x 8-12
Contracted:	Leg extensions	1 x 8-12

Hamstrings

Midrange & Stretch:	Stiff-legged deadlifts	2 x 8-12
Contracted:	Leg curls	2 x 8-12

Calves

Midrange:	Toes-pointed leg curls	1 x 12-20
Stretch:	Donkey calf raises	2 x 12-20
Contracted:	Standing calf raises	1 x 12-20

Upper chest

Midrange:	Incline presses	2 x 8-12
Stretch & Contracted:	Incline flyes	
	or	
	Incline cable flyes	1 x 8-12

Lower chest

Midrange:	Bench presses	2 x 8-12
Stretch & Contracted:	Decline flyes	
	or	
	Decline cable flyes	1 x 8-12

Triceps

Midrange:	Lying extensions	2 x 8-12
Stretch:	Overhead extensions	1 x 8-12
Contracted:	Dumbbell kickbacks	1 x 8-12

(continued on next page)

Locking out at the top of leg extensions is okay because that's the greatest point of stress in the exercise. But on exercises like the leg press or squat locking out gives you a rest, which isn't what you want.

LEE LABRADA
IRONMAN, September '91

Workout 2

Midback

Midrange:	Behind-the-neck chins	
	or	
	Behind-the-neck pulldowns	2 x 8-12
Stretch & Contracted:	Two-arm bent-over dumbbell rows	2 x 8-12

Lats

Midrange:	Chinups	
	or	
	Pulldowns to the front	2 x 8-12
Stretch:	Pullovers	1 x 8-12
Contracted:	Undergrip chins	1 x 8-12

Upper Traps

Stretch & Contracted:	Forward-lean shrugs	2 x 8-12

Deltoids

Midrange:	Behind-the-neck presses	2 x 8-12
Stretch:	Incline one-arm lateral raises	2 x 8-12
Contracted:	Lateral raises	1 x 8-12

Biceps

Midrange:	Barbell curls	2 x 8-12
Stretch:	Incline dumbbell curls	1 x 8-12
Contracted:	Concentration curls	1 x 8-12

Abdominals

Midrange & Lower Contracted:	Reverse crunches	1 x 10-20
Stretch:	Roman chair crunches	1 x 10-20
Upper Contracted:	Crunches	1 x 10-20

You've got to feel the muscle working to make the body respond.

BOB PARIS
Flawless

POF Every-Other-Day Split 2

Workout 1
Quadriceps

Midrange:	Front squats	
	or	
	Leg presses	2 x 10-15
Stretch:	Sissy squats	2 x 8-12
Contracted:	Leg extensions	1 x 8-12

Hamstrings

Midrange & Stretch:	Good mornings	2 x 8-12
Contracted:	Leg curls	2 x 8-12

Calves

Midrange:	Toes-pointed leg curls	1 x 12-20
Stretch:	Donkey calf raises	2 x 12-20
Contracted:	One-leg calf raises	2 x 12-20

Upper chest

Midrange:	Incline barbell presses	2 x 8-12
Stretch & Contracted:	Incline flyes	
	or	
	Incline cable flyes	2 x 8-12

Lower chest

Midrange:	Decline barbell presses	2 x 8-12
Stretch and Contracted:	Flat-bench flyes	
	or	
	Cable crossovers	2 x 8-12

Triceps

Midrange:	Lying dumbbell extensions	1 x 8-12
Stretch:	Overhead extensions	1 x 8-12
Contracted:	One-arm kickbacks	1 x 8-12

(continued on next page)

It took me 20 years to discover that two sets of each exercise during each workout is usually far better than four sets of each exercise; and then it took another 20 years for me to realize that one set of each exercise is usually better than two sets.

ARTHUR JONES
IRONMAN, July '93

Workout 2

Midback
Midrange:	Behind-the-neck chins	
	or	
	Pulldowns	2 x 8-12
Stretch:	One-arm dumbbell rows	2 x 8-12
Contracted:	Bent-over bent-arm laterals	2 x 8-12

Lats
Midrange:	Chinups or Pulldowns	2 x 8-12
Stretch:	Pullovers	1 x 8-12
Contracted:	Undergrip chins	
	or	
	Undergrip pulldowns	1 x 8-12

Deltoids
Midrange:	Behind-the-neck presses	2 x 8-12
Stretch:	Incline one-arm lateral raises	
	or	
	One-arm cable laterals	2 x 8-12
Contracted:	Wide-grip upright rows	1 x 8-12

Biceps
Midrange:	Preacher curls	2 x 8-12
Stretch:	Incline dumbbell curls	1 x 8-12
Contracted:	Spider curls	1 x 8-12

Forearm flexors
Stretch:	Incline wrist curls	1 x 8-12
Contracted:	Decline wrist curls	1 x 8-12

Forearm extensors
Midrange:	Hammer curls	1 x 8-12
Stretch:	Incline reverse wrist curls	1 x 8-12
Contracted:	Decline reverse wrist curls	1 x 8-12

Abdominals
Midrange & Lower Contracted:	Hanging kneeups	1 x 10-20
Stretch:	Roman chair crunches	1 x 10-20
Upper Contracted:	Cable crunches	1 x 10-20

Chapter 9
ULTRA-INTENSITY TRAINING: POF PRE-EX

Intensity is the primary prerequisite for muscle growth. The harder you train a muscle, the more likely it is to overcompensate with new size increases. Training intensely isn't that difficult in the beginning and early-intermediate stages of boybuilding, when heavy, compound, multi-joint exercises spur your muscles to new growth. Once you become more advanced, however, you must hit a muscle with as much direct, intense stress as possible for further growth. This can be difficult to achieve with conventional training methods due to weak links, as you saw in Chapter 7.

The best method for overcoming this weak-link problem is pre-exhaustion, a muscle-shocking method that can bring the more advanced bodybuilder large size increases—if it's used judiciously. So what would happen if you combine this ultra-intensity method with the efficiency of the Positions-of-Flexion strategy outlined in Chapter 8? You'd have one mega-mass-building regimen.

With the POF Pre-ex Routine you not only eliminate weak links, but you also work each muscle group through its three positions of flexion. This type of training really jolts every fiber to its core, and because of this heavy-duty effect you shouldn't use the POF Pre-ex Routine for more than a few weeks at a time. Beginners and early intermediates should avoid it completely.

In the ideal POF Pre-ex cycle you start out with a contracted-position movement because it keeps stress on the target muscle throughout the range of motion. This type of isolation with a high-stress component fatigues a large number of muscle fibers. From there you move immediately to a midrange movement to take advantage of the temporarily stronger weak link. After two

Leg extension by Tom Platz

of these supersets you finish off the bodypart with one to two sets of a stretch-position exercise. In other words, you cover the three positions—midrange, stretch and contracted—by doing a contracted-position exercise cycled with a midrange movement and then a stretch-position exercise.

Look at the routines at the end of this chapter, and you'll see that the majority of bodyparts follow this protocol. Of course, there are exceptions, but many of these actually make the pre-exhaustion method more advantageous and efficient. For example, the hamstrings workout is leg curls, a contracted-position movement, followed by stiff-legged deadlifts, a combination midrange-and-stretch-position exercise. Two-positions-in-one movements like the deadlift make pre-ex that

---

POF Pre-ex Tips

•Don't rest between the contracted-position movement and the midrange exercise.

•Always keep the weight under control—no jerking.

•Never do more than two pre-exhaustion cycles for any bodypart; one is usually plenty. A good rule of thumb is to do two pre-ex cycles for your weaker bodyparts and only one for your stronger muscle groups; however, you always want to consider your set total, which shouldn't exceed 25. Remember that this is an intensity technique—you're working harder, so do less for best results.

•Use the routines on an every-other-day-split schedule: Workout 1, Monday; rest Tuesday; Workout 2, Wednesday; rest Thursday; Workout 1, Friday; etc.

•Don't use POF Pre-ex for more than three to four weeks straight. You must respect this method's awesome intensity capabilities, or you'll undoubtedly overtrain and regress.

---

much more effective because you fatigue the muscle from two angles in less time.

Once you try POF Pre-ex, you'll immediately see why it's considered to be one of the best techniques for upping your muscle mass, and you'll also realize what real pain zone training is all about. Be prepared.

Massive back by Brian Buchanan

Never do today what you can't supersede tomorrow. Don't perform more exercises or more intensity than necessary to maintain an upward growth pattern.

VINCE GIRONDA
Unleashing the Wild Physique

POF Pre-ex Routine 1

Workout 1

Quadriceps

Contracted:	Leg extensions	1-2 x 8-12
	cycled with	
Midrange:	Squats	1-2 x 8-12
Stretch:	Sissy squats	1 x 8-12

Hamstrings

Contracted:	Lying leg curls	1 x 8-12
	cycled with	
Midrange & Stretch:	Stiff-legged deadlifts	1-2 x 8-12

Lower back

Contracted:	Hyperextensions	1-2 x 8-12

Calves

Contracted:	Standing calf raises	1-2 x 12-20
	cycled with	
Midrange:	Toes-pointed leg curls	1-2 x 12-20
Stretch:	Donkey calf raises	2 x 12-20

Upper chest

Stretch & Contracted:	Incline flyes* *or* incline cable flyes	1-2 x 8-12
	cycled with	
Midrange:	Incline presses	1-2 x 8-12

Lower chest

Stretch & Contracted:	Decline flyes* *or* decline cable flyes	2 x 8-12
	cycled with	
Midrange:	Barbell bench presses	2 x 8-12

Triceps**

Contracted:	Dumbbell kickbacks	1 x 8-12
	cycled with	
Midrange:	Close-grip bench presses	1 x 8-12
Stretch:	Overhead extensions	1 x 8-12

* Because there's no resistance in the contracted position, the dumbbell flye is not a true contracted-position movement; if you don't have cables, however, there's no true contracted-position chest exercise you can do in a home gym. Squeeze your pecs hard at the top of each flye repetition, and you'll get some contracted-position work.

** The triceps aren't hampered by weak links, but by pre-exhausting them with an isolation exercise you can force them to work harder on a compound movement with the help of a stronger bodypart. In this routine the chest helps the triceps during close-grip bench presses.

(continued on next page)

To be a really good bodybuilder, just creating mass is not enough. You need to create muscle shape, and this happens when you train every part of the muscle, at every angle possible, so that the entire muscle is stimulated and every bit of fiber is involved.

ARNOLD SCHWARZENEGGER
Encyclopedia of Modern Bodybuilding

Workout 2

Midback

Contracted:	Bent-arm bent-over laterals	1-2 x 8-12
	cycled with	
Midrange:	Behind-the-neck chins or pulldowns	1-2 x 8-12
Stretch:	One-arm bent-over dumbbell rows	1 x 8-12

Lats

Contracted:	Bent-over scapulae rotations *or* stiff-arm pulldowns	1-2 x 8-12
	cycled with	
Midrange:	Front chins *or* pulldowns	1-2 x 8-12
Stretch:	Barbell pullovers	1-2 x 8-12

Deltoids

Contracted:	Lateral raises	1-2 x 8-12
	cycled with	
Midrange:	Behind-the-neck presses	1-2 x 8-12
Stretch:	Incline one-arm lateral raises	1-2 x 8-12

Biceps*

Contracted:	Spider curls	1 x 8-12
	cycled with	
Midrange:	Undergrip chins *or* Undergrip pulldowns	1 x 8-12
Stretch:	Incline dumbbell curls	1 x 8-12

Abdominals

Upper Contracted:	Crunches	1 x 10-20
	cycled with	
Total Midrange & Lower Contracted:	Reverse crunches	1 x 10-20
Stretch:	Roman chair crunches	1 x 10-20

* The biceps aren't hampered by weak links, but by pre-exhausting them with an isolation exercise you can force them to work harder on a compound movement with the help of a stronger bodypart. In this routine the back pushes the biceps during undergrip chins.

Never terminate a set simply because a certain number of repetitions have been completed; a set is properly finished only when additional movement is utterly impossible.

ELLINGTON DARDEN, PH.D.
Strength Training by the Experts

POF Pre-ex Routine 2

Workout 1

Quadriceps

Contracted:	Leg extensions	1-2 x 8-12
	cycled with	
Midrange:	Front squats	
	or leg presses	1-2 x 8-12
Stretch:	Sissy squats	1 x 8-12

Hamstrings

Contracted:	Leg curls	1 x 8-12
	cycled with	
Midrange & Stretch:	Good mornings	1-2 x 8-12

Calves

Contracted:	Standing calf raises	1-2 x 12-20
	cycled with	
Midrange:	Toes-pointed leg curls	1-2 x 12-20
Stretch:	Donkey calf raises	2 x 12-20

Lower chest

Stretch & Contracted:	Flat-benchflyes*	
	or decline cable flyes	2 x 8-12
	cycled with	
Midrange:	Barbell bench presses	2 x 8-12

Upper chest

Stretch & Contracted:	Incline flyes*	
	or incline cable flyes	1-2 x 8-12
	cycled with	
Midrange:	Incline dumbbell presses	1-2 x 8-12

Triceps**

Contracted:	Dumbbell kickbacks	1 x 8-12
	cycled with	
Midrange:	Close-grip bench presses	1 x 8-12
Stretch:	One-arm overhead extensions	1 x 8-12

* Because there's no resistance in the contracted position, the dumbbell flye is not a true contracted-position movement; if you don't have cables, however, there's no true contracted-position chest exercise in a home gym. Squeeze your pecs hard at the top of each flye repetition, and you'll get some contracted-position work.

** The triceps aren't hampered by weak links, but by pre-exhausting them with an isolation exercise you can force this muscle group to work harder on a compound movement with the help of a stronger bodypart. In this routine the chest helps the triceps during close-grip bench presses.

(continued on next page)

I am a firm believer in the concept of working the muscles to their fullest range. Stretch your muscles to their full capacity and contract them as hard as you can.

FRANCO COLUMBU
3 More Reps

Workout 2

Midback

Contracted:	Bent-arm bent-over laterals *cycled with*	1-2 x 8-12
Midrange:	Behind-the-neck chins or pulldowns	1-2 x 8-12
Stretch:	One-arm bent-over dumbbell rows	1 x 8-12

Lats

Contracted:	Bent-over scapulae rotations or stiff-arm pulldowns *cycled with*	1-2 x 8-12
Midrange:	Wide-grip chins or pulldowns	1-2 x 8-12
Stretch:	Dumbbell pullovers	1 x 8-12

Deltoids

Contracted:	Lateral raises *cycled with*	1-2 x 8-12
Midrange:	Dumbbell presses	1-2 x 8-12
Stretch:	Incline one-arm lateral raises	1-2 x 8-12

Biceps*

Contracted:	Barbell concentration curls *cycled with*	1 x 8-12
Midrange:	Undergrip bent-over rows	1 x 8-12
Stretch:	Incline dumbbell curls	1 x 8-12

Abdominals

Upper Contracted:	Crunches *cycled with*	1 x 10-20
Midrange & Lower Contracted:	Hanging kneeups	1 x 10-20
Stretch:	Roman chair crunches	1 x 10-20

* The biceps aren't hampered by weak links, but by pre-exhausting them with an isolation exercise you can force this muscle group to work harder with a compound movement with the help of a stronger bodypart. In this routine the back pushes the biceps during undergrip bent-over rows.

Chapter 10
THE COMBINATION EQUATION

Is it possible to get really big in a home gym? Absolutely. Many great bodybuilders over the years have added muscle to their frames at home. If you've seen the film "Pumping Iron," you may have noticed that Mike Katz often trained in a home gym for his assault on the Mr. Universe—and he looked as big and wide as an aircraft carrier. Of course, you may also have noticed that he had a few people pushing him, not to mention the fact that he was training for the most important contest in his life, which would do wonders for anyone's motivation. Most of us don't have the luxury of all that inspiration.

The key to making big gains at home is undoubtedly tied to motivation, something that can be difficult to come by. At most commercial gyms, however, you get an atmosphere that's conducive to hard training, with great bodies strutting and pumping and the sounds of heavy iron being repped and racked. If these are the only things that get you motivated, you're out of luck when it comes to training at home.

But don't put your home equipment up for sale just yet. There's an option—an extremely productive option—that can give you the benefits of both worlds. The Combination Equation Routine, a strategy that combines home-gym and commercial-gym workouts. This is the ultimate in training variety, and it can spur your motivation and your intensity to the outer limits. Here are a couple of productive combo-training alternatives that work well:

Schedule 1
Saturday: commercial-gym, weak-point workout
Tuesday: home-gym, full-body workout
Thursday: home-gym, full-body workout

Schedule 2
Saturday: home-gym, weak-point workout
Tuesday: commercial-gym, full-body workout
Thursday: commercial-gym, full-body workout

The gains you'll make on this type of routine will be consistent, spectacular and rapid for the following reasons:

Recuperation. You get 48 hours between workouts during the week and then a necessary 72 hours after your grueling Saturday specialization session.

Variation. With two workout venues you've got a much broader choice of exercises, and the boredom factor doesn't rear its ugly head as often.

Inspiration. You get to work out alongside the bigger, better bodies at your commercial gym at least once a week.

Concentration. You get the home-gym benefit of increased mental focus at least once a week.

Integration. By stressing full-body workouts, you work the body as a complete system. For most intermediate bodybuilders this provides for better recovery and growth.

Intensification. Because you only work a few bodyparts on Saturday, this weak-point specialization day allows you to blast your lagging muscles into submission with more intensity than they usually get.

Adaptation. If you happen to miss one of the full-body workouts during the week, you can get one in on Saturday and skip the specialization. Two full-body workouts during the week will stimulate plenty of growth.

As you can see, the Combination Equation strategy is actually a three-days-per-week routine with a twist—two full-body workouts during the week plus one weak-point session on Saturday. Many of the routines in previous chapters will adapt easily to this schedule, and you can incorporate them with great success. To load even more training tactics into your bodybuilding arsenal, let's plug in a different regimen, a variation on one of the best mass-building methods around, POF.

POF, as you'll recall, is about efficiency in the gym and working each muscle group through its three positions of flexion—midrange, stretch and contracted. While it's true that you should train all three positions for each muscle group for full, complete development, you don't have to train all three on the same day. And if you're a hardgainer you should never do it. (Note: These folks can take advantage of POF's mass-building capabilities with the Hardgainer's POF Routine outlined in *IRONMAN's Critical Mass.* This is basically the Tuesday and Thursday workouts listed at the end of this chapter without the Saturday specialization session.)

On Tuesday you do a midrange exercise followed by a stretch-position movement for each bodypart, and then on Thursday you do the midrange movement again but this time follow it with a contracted-position exercise. You still work all three position but over two workouts, and you give more emphasis to the important midrange movement.

If you're not an extreme hardgainer, however, you can stand a bit more work, which is where the Combination Equation Routine comes in. You get one extra workout a week for your slow-to-grow bodyparts, and there's no holding back on that session as you blast your weak points through all three positions of flexion.

Analyze the routines at the end of this chapter, and you'll see that the Combination Equation has the capability to be one of the most productive size-building strategies around. If you have a home gym and there's a commercial gym nearby that's calling your name, give this tactic a try. You'll grow to love it.

Combination Equation Tips

•On Saturday, your specialization day, don't work more than two large bodyparts or one large and two small bodyparts. Chest, lats, midback and quads are large bodyparts; the small ones include biceps, triceps, delts, hamstrings, calves, forearms and upper traps.

•On Saturday work the weakest of your weak bodyparts first, then second weakest and so on unless you're working arms; always train biceps, triceps and forearms last.

•Your Saturday workouts don't have to be for weak points. You can also train minor bodyparts that aren't included in your full-body sessions, such as forearms, upper traps and/or brachialis (see Routine 2).

•Try to keep your Saturday workout to under an hour.

•On commercial-gym days you may want to use equipment that you don't have in your home gym. For example, instead of regular barbell curls you could do machine preacher curls. Or instead of dumbbell flyes you could do cable crossovers. This type of substitution will keep boredom at bay for even longer periods.

•The soleus muscles can give your calves more bulk—they lie under your gastrocnemius on each leg and fill out the lower-leg area as they become more developed. You work the midrange of these muscles with toes-pointed leg curls, which also work the

---

gastrocs, and the stretch position with donkey calf raises, which also target the gastrocs. To work the soleus' contracted position, however, you need a seated calf machine, which you don't often find in home gyms. For this reason you should do seated calf raises at almost all of your commercial-gym workouts.

•On Monday work your upper chest first, then your lower chest. On Friday reverse the order and work your lower chest first, then your upper chest. This gives priority to each chest area once a week.

•Flip-flop the order for midback and lats just as you do for your upper and lower chests. Again, this give them equal priority.

•Because of all the indirect stimulation your arms receive from pressing and pulling movements, you shouldn't waste recovery ability on training the three positions for biceps and triceps unless they really need the work. Usually, one exercise for each of these muscle groups will suffice, and although there are midrange movements listed in the routine, feel free to use a stretch- or contracted-position movement instead. (The workout in chapter 9 indicates substitution exercises.)

•Do one or two warmup sets for each midrange movement.

•Work all sets to failure during an intense-training phase.

If your enthusiasm is waning, a change from home training to gym training could be the answer.

VINCE GIRONDA
Unleashing the Wild Physique

Combination Equation Routine 1

Tuesday: Full body, home gym

Quadriceps

Midrange:	Squats	1 x 8-12
Stretch:	Sissy squats	1 x 8-12

Hamstrings

Midrange & Stretch:	Stiff-legged deadlifts	1 x 8-12

Calves

Midrange:	Toes-pointed leg curls	1 x 12-20
Stretch:	Donkey calf raises	1 x 12-20

Upper chest

Midrange:	Incline presses	1 x 8-12
Stretch & Contracted:	Incline flyes*	1 x 8-12

Lower chest

Midrange:	Bench presses	1 x 8-12

Midback

Midrange:	Behind-the-neck chins	1 x 8-12
Stretch & Contracted:	Bent-over dumbbell rows	1 x 8-12

Lats

Midrange:	Front chins	1 x 8-12
Stretch:	Pullovers	1 x 8-12

Deltoids

Midrange:	Behind-the-neck presses	1 x 8-12
Stretch:	Incline one-arm lateral raises	1 x 8-12

Triceps

Midrange:	Lying triceps extensions	1 x 8-12

Biceps

Midrange:	Barbell curls	1 x 8-12

Abdominals

Midrange & Lower Contracted:	Reverse crunches	1 x 10-20
Stretch:	Roman chair crunches	1 x 10-20

* Because there's no resistance in the contracted position, the dumbbell flye is not a true contracted-position movement; if you don't have cables, however, there's no contracted-position chest exercise you can do in a home gym. Squeeze your pecs hard at the top of each flye repetition, and you'll get some contracted-position work.

(continued on next page)

Don't let yourself get bored, for boredom is the mother of failure.

ARNOLD SCHWARZENEGGER
3 More Reps

Thursday: Full body, home gym

Quadriceps

Midrange:	Squats	1 x 8-12
Contracted:	Leg extensions	1 x 8-12

Hamstrings

Midrange & Stretch:	Stiff-legged deadlifts	1 x 8-12
Contracted:	Leg curls	1 x 8-12

Calves

Midrange:	Toes-pointed leg curls	1 x 8-12
Contracted:	One-leg calf raises	1 x 12-20

Lower chest

Midrange:	Bench presses	1 x 8-12
Stretch & Contracted:	Decline flyes*	1 x 8-12

Upper chest

Midrange:	Incline presses	1 x 8-12

Lats

Midrange:	Front chins	1 x 8-12
Conracted:	Undergrip bent-over rows	1 x 8-12

Midback

Midrange:	Behind-the-neck chins	1 x 8-12
Contracted:	Bent-arm bent-over lateral raises	1 x 8-12

Deltoids

Midrange:	Behind-the-neck presses	1 x 8-12
Contracted:	Lateral raises	1 x 8-12

Triceps

Midrange:	Lying triceps extensions	1 x 8-12

Biceps

Midrange:	Barbell curls	1 x 8-12

Abdominals

Total Midrange & Lower Contracted:	Reverse crunches	1 x 10-20
Upper Contracted:	Crunches	1 x 10-20

* Because there's no resistance in the contracted position, the dumbbell flye is not a true contracted-position movement; if you don't have cables, however, there's no contracted-position chest exercise you can do in a home gym. Squeeze your pecs hard at the top of each flye repetition, and you'll get some contracted-position work.

Continued on next page

The evidence always points back to the same basic conclusions—more than three weekly workouts, or more than two sets of any one exercise in the same workout, or more than a total of four hours of weekly training will almost always result in overtraining and a reduction in the production of results.

ARTHUR JONES
Nautilus Training Bulletin No. 2

Saturday: Weak bodyparts, commercial gym

Thighs

Midrange:	Leg presses	2 x 8-12
Stretch:	Sissy squats	2 x 8-12
Contracted:	Leg extensions	1 x 8-12

Soleus

Contracted:	Seated calf raises	2 x 8-12

Upper chest

Midrange:	Incline Smith machine presses	2 x 8-12
Stretch & Contracted:	Incline cable flyes	1 x 8-12

Lower chest

Midrange:	Decline machine presses	2 x 8-12
Stretch & Contracted:	Cable crossovers	1 x 8-12

Why does a bodybuilder get bigger muscles than a construction worker? The reason is progressive overload.

CORY EVERSON
Superflex

Combination Equation Routine 2

Tuesday: Full body, commercial gym

Quadriceps
Midrange:	Smith machine squats	1 x 8-12
Stretch:	Sissy squats	1 x 8-12

Hamstrings
Midrange & Stretch:	Stiff-legged deadlifts	1 x 8-12

Calves
Midrange:	Toes-pointed leg curls	1 x 12-20
Stretch:	Donkey calf raises	1 x 12-20

Soleus
Contracted:	Seated calf raises	2 x 8-12
Stretch:	Donkey calf machine	1 x 12-20

Upper chest
Midrange:	Incline dumbbell presses	1 x 8-12
Stretch & Contracted:	Incline cable flyes	1 x 8-12

Lower chest
Midrange:	Decline presses	1 x 8-12

Midback
Midrange:	Behind-the-neck pulldowns	1 x 8-12
Stretch:	Close parallel-grip (V-handle) cable rows	1 x 8-12

Lats
Midrange:	Front pulldowns	1 x 8-12
Stretch & Contracted:	Machine pullovers	1 x 8-12

Deltoids
Midrange:	Behind-the-neck presses	1 x 8-12
Stretch:	One-arm cable laterals	1 x 8-12

Triceps
Midrange:	Lying triceps extensions	1 x 8-12

Biceps
Midrange:	Machine preacher curls	1 x 8-12

Abdominals
Midrange & Lower Contracted:	Reverse crunches	1 x 10-20
Stretch:	Roman chair crunches	1 x 10-20

Continued on next page

Essentially, the amount of weight you use for your exercises will determine your muscle size. When size is the goal, I rest a little longer so as to allow me to handle respectable poundages.

FRANK ZANE
3 More Reps

Thursday: Full body, commercial gym

Quadriceps

Midrange:	Smith machine squats	1 x 8-12
Contracted:	Leg extensions	1 x 8-12

Hamstrings

Midrange & Stretch:	Stiff-legged deadlifts	1 x 8-12
Contracted:	Leg curls	1 x 8-12

Calves

Contracted:	Standing calf raises	1 x 12-20

Soleus

Contracted:	Seated calf raises	1 x 8-12

Lower chest

Midrange:	Decline presses	1 x 8-12
Stretch & Contracted:	Cable flyes	1 x 8-12

Upper chest

Midrange:	Incline dumbbell presses	1 x 8-12

Lats

Midrange:	Front pulldowns	1 x 8-12
Stretch & Conracted:	Machine pullovers	1 x 8-12

Midback

Midrange:	Behind-the-neck pulldowns	1 x 8-12
Contracted:	Bent-over bent-arm lateral raises	1 x 8-12

Deltoids

Midrange:	Behind-the-neck presses	1 x 8-12
Contracted:	Lateral raises	1 x 8-12

Triceps

Midrange:	Lying triceps extensions	1 x 8-12

Biceps

Midrange:	Machine preacher curls	1 x 8-12

Abdominals

Total Midrange & Lower Contracted:	Reverse crunches	1 x 10-20
Upper Contracted:	Ab machine crunches	1 x 10-20

(continued on next page)

Success in bodybuilding requires discipline and hard work; but discipline and hard work alone aren't a guarantee of success. You must also use your head. Study! Plan! Experiment! Evaluate!

CLARENCE BASS
Ripped

Saturday: Weak bodyparts, home gym

Triceps

Midrange:	Close-grip bench presses	2 x 8-12
Stretch:	Overhead extensions	2 x 8-12
Contracted:	One-arm kickbacks	1 x 8-12

Biceps

Midrange:	Barbell curls	2 x 8-12
Stretch:	Incline dumbbell curls	2 x 8-12
Contracted:	Concentration curls	1 x 8-12

Forearm flexors

Stretch:	Incline wrist curls	1 x 8-12
Contracted:	Behind-the-back wrist curls	1 x 8-12

Forearm extensors

Midrange:	Hammer curls	1 x 8-12
Stretch:	Incline reverse wrist curls	1 x 8-12
Contracted:	Decline reverse wrist curls	1 x 8-12

AFTERWORD

Variety. Intensity. Overload. These are interesting, motivational bodybuilding buzzwords, but the most important term of all in the bodybuilding vernacular is "effort." None of the routines in this book will work if you don't. Whichever program you choose, you have to push your workouts into the ozone if you want to make real gains.

Don't be afraid of all-out effort. When you're in a high-intensity phase, take all sets other than warmups to the limit and then some. How do you want to look when you're at your physical best? How will you feel when you reach this goal? Keep the image of your ideal physique in mind, and use this image and emotion to spur you on to bigger and better gains and to force your muscles into and through the pain zone.

Remember that in bodybuilding, as in other areas of life, there's no free lunch. You have to work for what you get, and the harder you work, the more results you'll reap. Train hard and intelligently, and the routines in this book will help you take your size and strength above and beyond your greatest expectations.

Effort by Shawn Ray

APPENDIX

Alternating lunges *(quadriceps, hamstrings, buttocks)*. Stand erect with a barbell across your shoulders. Step out about two feet in front of you with your right foot, bend your right knee until you're in a lunge position and your left knee touches the floor. From here push back to the starting position (feet together) with your right leg and repeat with your left. Continue alternating legs throughout the set. Tip: For a variation of this movement try reverse lunges. Step back with the nonworking leg while slowly bending the working leg. Touch the knee of the nonworking leg to the floor, drive back up to the starting position and repeat with the other leg.

Barbell concentration curls *(biceps)*. Bend at your waist and take a shoulder-width grip on a barbell. Raise your torso until it's just below parallel to the ground and the plates on the bar clear the floor. Curl the bar up to your nose, hold for a count of two and return to the starting position. Tip: Try different hand spacings to enhance the biceps contraction.

Barbell curls *(biceps)*. Stand upright with a loaded barbell at arm's length. Slowly curl the bar up to your shoulders without swinging your body. Some upper-arm movement is okay, but don't let it get out of hand. Tip: Lean slightly forward to keep resistance on the biceps at the top of the movement. Alternate exercises: seated dumbbell curls, alternate dumbbell curls.

Behind-the-neck chins *(midback and latissimus dorsi)*. Take a slightly wider-than-shoulder-width grip on the chinning bar and pull yourself up until the back of your neck touches the bar. Lower and repeat. Tip: At the top make sure your shoulder blades are together so the movement hits your middle back.

Reverse curl by Danny Padilla

Alternate exercise: behind-the-neck pulldowns.

Behind-the-neck presses *(deltoids)*. Take a loaded barbell off a rack and onto your shoulders as if you were about to do squats. Sit on a bench, plant your feet on the floor and press the barbell overhead. Lower the bar to the back of your neck and repeat. Tip: Don't pause at the bottom. Also, try a set without locking out on any of the reps. Alternate exercises: standing barbell presses, seated dumbbell presses.

Bench dips *(triceps)*. Place two exercise benches parallel to each other and about four feet apart. Kneel between them, facing one and away from the other. Reach behind you, grab the inner edge of the bench you're facing away from and support yourself with locked arms as you rest the heels of your feet on the other bench. Unlock your arms and lower yourself until your upper arms dip below parallel to the floor, then reverse the movement and ram yourself back up to the starting position. Tip: Make it a point to flex your triceps hard at the top of each rep.

Bench presses *(chest)*. Recline on a bench with a loaded bar on the racks. Take a slightly wider-than-shoulder-width grip on the bar, lift it off of the racks and lower to your middle-chest area. Without pausing, ram the bar back to arm's length and repeat. When doing this exercise, you should always have someone standing by in case you miss. Tip: To get the most pec development from this movement, keep your elbows out away from your body. Alternate exercise: dumbbell bench presses.

Bent-over bent-arm lateral raises *(midback)*. Take a dumbbell in each hand and bend at the waist until your torso is parallel to the floor. Keep a slight bend in your elbows, raise the dumbbells out until they're parallel to the floor or higher. Squeeze your scapulae for two seconds, then lower and repeat. You can do these standing or seated. Tip: Don't throw the weights up; try to feel your midback muscles contracting.

Bent-over barbell rows *(midback)*. Bend at your waist, grab a loaded barbell with a slightly wider-than-shoulder-width grip and pull the bar to your lower rib cage. Keep your elbows angled out away from your sides and don't raise your torso above parallel to the floor. Tip: Try a double-pump action at the top of each rep to ensure that you get a peak contraction in your midback. Alternate exercises: one-arm dumbbell rows (a better choice for those people who have low-back problems), incline dumbbell rows (performed facedown on an incline bench).

Bent-over scapulae rotations *(latissimus dorsi)*. Take a dumbbell in each hand and bend at the waist until your torso is parallel to the floor. Keeping a slight bend in your elbows, raise the dumbbells up and back until your arms are past your torso. This looks like the finish position of a kickback only your arms are slightly bent. Squeeze your lats hard for two seconds, lower the dumbbells and repeat. Alternate exercise: stiff-arm pulldowns

Breathing squats *(quadriceps)*. Take a loaded bar off of a rack and position it at about the midtrap line across your back. (You might want to place a towel across your upper back before shouldering the bar.) The bar will be pushing against your rear-delt heads and should feel somewhat low but very stable. Place your feet just wider than shoulder width apart with your toes angled slightly outward. Take a couple of breaths, and then inhale as you begin your descent. Keep your back flat—no rounding—and your eyes focused straight ahead. Don't look up or your lower back will arch. Also, keep your torso as upright as possible. The descent should take two to three seconds. When the tops of your thighs dip just below parallel to the floor, explode, but don't bounce, out of the squat and ram the weight back to the starting position as you exhale. Take three deep breaths and start your second descent as you inhale for the fourth time. You'll never take less than three deep breaths between reps, and after about your 10th rep you'll probably need six to 10 breaths to keep going.

Chinups *(latissimus dorsi)*. Grab a chinup bar with a slightly wider-than-shoulder-width grip. Pull yourself up without arching your lower back too much and touch your upper chest to the bar—or at least come close to this position. Lower slowly and repeat. Tip: Keep pumping out the reps in rapid-fire fashion, but don't let your body swing. You can rest your feet on a bench to prevent this swinging, if necessary. Alternate exercise: pulldowns.

Close-grip bench presses *(triceps)*. Do these just like regular bench presses, but use a grip that puts your thumbs about eight inches apart.

Close-grip upright rows *(upper trapeziuses and deltoids)*. Take an overhand grip on a barbell with your thumbs about six inches apart and stand erect. Pull the bar up to chest level while keeping it close to your body. Lower and repeat.

Concentration curls *(biceps)*. Bend at your waist and grab a dumbbell with one hand. Raise your torso until it's just below parallel to the ground and the plates on the dumbbell clear the floor. Curl the 'bell up to your front-delt head without moving your upper arm, hold for a count of two and return to the starting position. Tip: Rotate your little finger up at the top of the movement for a better biceps contraction.

Crunches *(abdominals)*. Recline on your back on the floor with your lower legs supported on an exercise bench (legs bent at a 90-degree angle). Roll up until your upper back is off of the floor, blow the air out of your lungs and contract your abs hard. Uncurl your body, inhale and repeat. Tip: Keep your lower back against the ground at all times.

Deadlifts *(quadriceps, lower back, glutes, upper back)*. With a loaded barbell bar on the floor in front of you and your feet about shoulder width apart, squat down until your thighs are just below parallel to the ground. Grab the bar with a shoulder-width over-under grip—your hands on the outsides of your legs, one hand holding the bar with an overgrip, the other taking it with a curl grip. This grip will help prevent the bar from rolling out of your hands. Keep your head up and your back flat. Take a deep breath and then stand erect as you exhale, driving with your hips and legs as far as you can go. Your lower-back muscles should come into play as the bar passes your knees. When you get to the top position, don't lean back, but do pull your shoulders out of the slump-shoulder posture. From there lower the bar slowly back to the floor as you inhale. Take two to three deep breaths and repeat. Tip: You can grip the bar on the inside of your legs and use a wider foot placement if it's more comfortable.

Decline flyes *(lower chest)*. Set one end of your bench up on your calf block, making sure that it's sturdy and won't flip over. Grab a dumbbell in each hand and recline on the bench with your head at the lower end. Press the dumbbells over your chest and then, with your elbows slightly bent, lower the dumbbells down and back. When you feel a good stretch in your pecs, raise the dumbbells up over your chest as if you were hugging a tree and repeat. Tip: Squeeze your pecs at the top for two seconds.

Decline reverse wrist curls *(forearm extensors)*. Set one end of your bench on your calf block, take a close, overhand grip on a loaded barbell and sit at the low end of the bench, resting your forearms on the low end with your hands hanging off. With the angle at your elbows less than 90 degrees for better extensor contraction, curl the bar up as high as possible and flex the forearm extensor muscles on the tops of your lower arms. Lower and repeat.

Decline wrist curls *(forearm flexors)*. Set one end of your bench on your calf block, take a close, underhand grip on a loaded barbell and sit at the low end of the bench, resting your forearms on the low end with your hands hanging off the bench. Keeping the angle at your elbows at less than 90 degrees for better flexor contraction, curl the bar up as high as possible and flex your inner forearm muscles. Lower and repeat.

Dips (elbows in) *(triceps)*. Get up on your dipping bars with your arms locked. From there bend your arms, keeping them close to your body and holding your head up. When you reach the bottom, reverse your direction, drive back to the top position and repeat. Tip: Flex your triceps hard in the top position of every rep. Alternate exercise: bench dips.

Dips (elbows out) *(chest)*. Support yourself on your dipping bars with locked arms. Tuck your chin on your chest and lower slowly to the bottom position, keeping your elbows out away from your body. You should feel a stretch in your pectorals.

Without pausing, drive back to the top position. Alternate exercise: decline bench press.

Donkey calf raises *(calves)*. Bend at your waist, holding your torso and thighs at a 90 degree angle, and rest your forearms on a table, high bench or racked barbell bar with the balls of your feet up on your calf block. Have your training partner sit on your hips while you do calf raises until failure. Tip: If you train solo, you can still do donkeys by hanging a weight around your hips with a weight belt.

Feet-elevated pushups *(chest)*. This is a very effective exercise, but there's really no way to add weight. This means that when you reach the upper-rep range, you may want to switch to bench presses. Get in the standard pushup position but with your feet elevated on a bench. Position your hands a little wider than shoulder width, keep your elbows out and touch your chest to the floor. If you hold your head up, you'll work more of the middle and lower chest. Tip: Place something the thickness of a phone book under each hand in order to get a better stretch in your pectorals (You can buy pushup bars at most sporting goods stores.) Alternate exercises: parallel-bar dips (elbows out), bench presses.

Flat-bench flyes *(chest)*. Grab a dumbbell in each hand and recline on a flat bench. Press the dumbbells over your chest and then, with your elbows slightly bent, lower them down and back. When you feel a good stretch in your pecs, raise the dumbbells up over your chest again as if you were hugging a tree and repeat. Tip: Squeeze your pecs at the top for two seconds to get a slight peak-contraction effect.

Forward-lean shrugs *(upper traps)*. Take an overhand, shoulder-width grip on a loaded barbell and stand erect. Lean forward slightly and shrug your shoulders up toward your ears as high as possible. Hold for a count of two, lower and repeat.

Freehand calf raises *(calves)*. Begin doing calf raises—using both feet—in rapid fashion until your calves "burn out." Perform the reps as fast as possible without using momentum, and be prepared for a few seconds of cramping. Tip: Lean forward against a wall for a better stretch.

Front squats *(quadriceps)*. Do these like regular squats with your heel on a two-by-four-inch block, but instead of putting the bar on the back of your neck, place it across your front delts, crossing your arms to grip the bar at opposite shoulders and holding your elbows high so the bar doesn't roll.

Good mornings *(hamstrings, lower back)*. Place a loaded barbell across the backs of your shoulders as if you were going to do squats. With your knees locked, bend forward holding your back flat until your torso is parallel to the floor. Look straight ahead throughout the movement in order to keep your balance. Alternate exercise: stiff-legged deadlifts.

Hanging kneeups *(abdominals)*. Hang from a chinup bar, cross your legs at the ankles and pull your knees into your chest as you roll your hips forward and up. Hold for a count of two, lower and repeat. Tip: These are difficult, so if you're having trouble with form, stick to reverse crunches and progress to reverse crunches on a slant board before you try hanging kneeups again. Alternate exercise: reverse crunches.

Hammer curls *(forearm extensors, biceps, brachialis)*. Do these like dumbbell curls, but perform the entire movement with your thumbs up.

Incline barbell presses *(upper chest)*. Recline on a 35 degree incline bench with a loaded barbell on the racks behind you. Take a slightly wider-than-shoulder-width grip on the bar, palms facing forward, and unrack the weight. From this arms-extended position over your chest, lower the bar to your clavicles and without pausing drive it back to the top and repeat. Tip: To get a real burn in your upper pecs, don't lock out at the top of your reps; simply drive up to the two-thirds position and then repeat. Alternate exercise: incline dumbbell presses.

Incline dumbbell curls *(biceps)*. Recline on a 45 degree incline bench with a dumbbell in each hand. From this biceps-stretched position curl the dumbbells up to your shoulders simultaneously with as little upper-arm movement as possible. Lower to the stretch position and with a quick reversal of direction—no pause—repeat. Tip: Supinating your hands will help contract the biceps more fully. To do this, start with your palms facing each other. As you curl the dumbbells, begin to turn your palms up. In the top position try to twist your little fingers as high as possible. Lower and repeat.

Incline dumbbell presses *(upper chest).* Use a 35-degree incline bench for these. Clean the dumbbells up to your shoulders, recline on the bench and start pressing. Drive the dumbbells up to arm's length above your eyes. Keep your elbows away from your body on the way down. Tip: Try one set with your palms facing each other and the next set with your palms facing forward for different leverage. Also, always keep your lower back flat against the bench. Alternate exercise: incline barbell presses.

Incline dumbbell rows *(midback).* Take a dumbbell in each hand and straddle an incline bench, facing the bench. Bend over, with your chest at the top of the incline, and let your arms hang straight down from your torso. Pull the dumbbells up into your front-delt heads with your upper arms angled away from your body. Squeeze your scapulae together for a count of two, lower and repeat. Alternate exercise: bent-over two-arm dummbell rows.

Incline flyes *(upper chest).* Take a dumbbell in each hand and recline on a 35 degree incline bench. Press the dumbbells up over your chest, and then, with your elbows slightly bent, lower the dumbbells down and back until they're on the same plane as your deltoids. Using pec power alone, raise the 'bells back to the starting position as though you were hugging a tree, then repeat. Tip: Flex your upper-chest muscles at the top of every rep.

Incline one-arm lateral raises *(deltoids).* Sit sideways on an incline bench, and lean your shoulder against the bench while you work your other shoulder with a one-arm lateral raise. The incline allows the delt to get a full stretch in the bottom position. Tip: Keep the dumbbell handle parallel to the floor at all times. Alternate exercise: one-arm cable laterals.

Incline reverse wrist curls *(forearm extensors).* With one end of your bench up on your calf block take a close, overhand grip on a loaded barbell and sit on the high end of the bench, resting your forearms on the high end with your hands hanging off the bench. Make sure that the angle at your elbow is less than 90 degrees, and curl the bar up until your hands are almost perpendicular to the floor. Lower all the way down, then quickly reverse direction at the bottom and repeat.

Incline wrist curls *(forearm flexors)*. With one end of your bench up on your calf block take a close, underhand grip on a loaded barbell and sit on the high end of the bench, resting your forearms on the high end with your hands hanging off the bench. Make sure that the angle at your elbow is less than 90 degrees, and curl the bar up until your hands are almost perpendicular to the floor. Lower all the way down, then quickly reverse direction at the bottom and repeat.

Kickbacks *(triceps)*. Take a dumbbell in each hand and bend at the waist until your torso is parallel to the floor. With your upper arms next to your sides and your arms bent at 90 degree angles, extend your forearms back and contract your triceps (your arms should be higher than your torso in the top position). Lower the dumbbells, keeping your upper arms stationary, and repeat. Tip: Try one set with your palms facing your thighs and one set with your palms facing up. Alternate exercise: one-arm triceps pushdowns.

Lateral raises *(deltoids)*. Take a dumbbell in each hand and stand erect with the dumbbells in front of your thighs and your palms facing each other. Raise the dumbbells out from your sides with slightly bent arms until the 'bells are at shoulder level. You should feel a contraction in the side-delt heads. Lower and repeat. Tip: Watch the position of the dumbbells; keep them parallel to the floor. If the front of the dumbbell is higher than the rear, your front deltoid will get the brunt of the work. Alternate exercise: upright rows.

Leg curls *(hamstrings)*. Load your leg curl apparatus, lie facedown on the bench and place the back of your lower legs against the roller pads. From there curl your lower legs up, keeping your feet flexed toward your shins, until the pads touch your buttocks. Hold for a count of two, lower and repeat. Tip: Support your upper body on your elbows to keep yourself from putting too much hip movement into the exercise.

Leg extensions *(quadriceps)*. Load your leg extension apparatus, sit down and hook your feet under the roller pads— your knees should be bent at 90 degree angles. With your torso at a 90 degree angle to your thighs, extend your lower legs until your knees lock and your quadriceps contract. Hold this position for a count of two, lower and repeat.

Lying dumbbell triceps extensions *(triceps)*. Take a dumbbell in each hand and lie back on a flat bench. With the dumbbells over your chest in the arm-extended position and your palms facing each other, bend your elbows back, lowering the 'bells in an arc to your ears while keeping your elbows as close together as possible (and without hitting yourself in the face with the dumbbells). Then drive them back up to the beginning position and repeat. Tip: You can let your upper arms move somewhat to enhance the triceps contraction. Alternate exercise: lying triceps extensions.

Lying triceps extensions *(triceps)*. Lie back on a bench and press a loaded barbell up over your chest with a close grip (eight inches between thumbs). While keeping your upper arms as stationary as possible, lower the bar back and touch it either to your forehead or to the bench behind your head, whichever is more comfortable, while keeping your elbows as close together as possible. Drive the bar back over your chest in an arc and repeat. Tip: Keep your upper arms parallel and angled slightly back throughout the movement. Alternate exercise: Lying dumbbell triceps extensions.

Military presses *(deltoids)*. Clean a loaded barbell bar to your shoulders. From there keep your torso as upright as possible and press the bar overhead. Lower to neck level and repeat. Tip: Try going only two-thirds of the way up on each rep for continuous tension on your delts.

One-arm bent-over dumbbell rows *(back)*. Take a dumbbell in one hand and bend at the waist with the arm that's holding the weight hanging straight down and your other arm supported on the bench. Pull the dumbbell up to your shoulder, bending your elbow and keeping your palm facing inward (toward the bench) and your upper arm angled out away from your torso. Lower and repeat. Work each side separately. Tip: Squeeze your middle back hard at the top of each rep. Alternate exercise: bent-over barbell rows.

One-arm nonsupport concentration curls *(biceps)*. Take a dumbbell in one hand, bend at the waist with your arm hanging straight down. Curl the dumbbell up to your shoulder, keeping your torso and upper arm as motionless as possible. Lower and repeat. Work each arm separately. Tip: Try the supination technique mentioned in the description for incline dumbbell curls on these as well, and hold each rep at the top for a two-second peak contraction. Alternate exercise: barbell concentration curls.

One-leg calf raises *(calves)*. Hold a dumbbell in your hand on the same side as the calf you're working or secure a sufficient amount of poundage around your waist with a weight belt. Grasp one of your bench uprights with your free hand for support, place the ball of your foot on your calf block and begin doing repetitions. Tip: Try to rise with more pressure on the big-toe side of the foot for inner-calf stimulation. Alternate exercise: standing calf raises.

One-leg squats *(quadriceps, buttocks, hamstrings)*. Don't pass this movement off as an easy exercise. It's tough and will jolt your thighs into rapid growth when pushed to failure. Raise your bench press racks to about shoulder height and place a bar across them. Then stand up on the bench, balance on one leg while holding onto the bar for stability and squat, letting your resting leg dangle freely beside the bench. Tip: Try to keep your torso upright, and when you're able to get 15 reps, add weight by holding a dumbbell or barbell plate in your hand on the same side of your body as your working leg. Alternate exercises: barbell squats, front squats.

Overhead extensions *(triceps)*. This is best done with an EZ-curl bar. Grab the bar in the middle position with your thumbs about six inches apart. Press the bar overhead, then bend your elbows back, lowering the bar behind your head while keeping your upper arms as stationary as possible. When you reach the stretch position, quickly reverse the movement—but don't bounce—and press the bar back overhead.

Preacher curls *(biceps)*. Take a shoulder-width grip on a barbell and position yourself over an angled preacher bench. The top of the bench should be almost touching your armpits, and your body should be upright, with your chest pressed into the back of the pad. Lower the bar until your arms are extended and then curl it back up to your nose. Lower and repeat. Tip: Try different hand spacings for slightly different effects.

Pullovers *(latissimus dorsi)*. Recline on a flat bench with your head hanging off of one end and a loaded EZ-curl bar on the floor behind you. Grab the bar with a shoulder-width grip and your palms facing up. With your arms bent, pull the bar up and over your head to your chest, keeping it about two inches from your face. Touch the bar to your upper chest, lower back to the floor and repeat. Tip: Hook your feet around the legs of the bench for better stability. You can also do this exercise with stiff arms, but don't lower the bar too far past the level of the bench or you could injure your shoulders.

Reverse crunches *(abdominals)*. Lie on the ground, bend your knees and cross your feet at the ankles. Open your legs until the sides of your thighs are almost touching the floor. With your arms at your sides and your hands flat on the ground, curl your knees toward your chest. Your hips will come off the ground a few inches as you "roll up" in the finish position. Lower your legs, touch your feet to the floor and repeat. Tip: Blow the air out of your lungs in the finish position to get a more intense ab contraction. Alternate exercise: hanging kneeups.

Reverse curls *(forearm extensors, biceps, brachialis)*. Do regular standing barbell curls but use an overhand grip on the bar instead of an undergrip. This exercise will work the entire forearm area—primarily the extensors—plus the brachialis, a muscle located between the biceps and triceps on the outer, upper arm. Tip: You can also use an EZ-curl bar on these for a slightly different effect.

Roman chair crunches *(abdominals)*. Position yourself on a Roman chair—with your legs bent at 90 degree angles and your feet hooked under the footpads—and lower yourself back until your torso is just below parallel to the floor. As soon as you reach this position, curl, or crunch, your torso up and contract your abdominals. Lower and repeat. Tip: Remember that this is a crunch, not a situp; Roman chair situps involve your hip flexors to a large extent.

Seated dumbbell curls *(biceps)*. Sit on the end of a bench with a dumbbell in each hand. With your palms facing forward, curl the dumbbells up simultaneously until they reach your shoulders. Lower and repeat. Tip: Supinate your hands. To do this, start the movement with your palms facing each other, and as you curl, rotate your hands, turning the little fingers up when you reach the top. Alternate exercise: barbell curls.

Seated dumbbell presses *(deltoids)*. Sit on the end of a bench and clean a pair of dumbbells to your shoulders. With the weights resting on your shoulders, press them both overhead while keeping your palms facing forward. Try to stay upright, with as little back arch as possible. Lower slowly. Tip: You can also try alternate dumbbell presses—lowering one dumbbell as you raise the other. This will keep your cheating to a minimum. Alternate exercises: behind-the-neck presses, military presses.

Sissy squats *(quadriceps)*. Hold onto an upright with one hand and bend your knees while keeping your thighs and torso on the same plane; that is don't bend at the waist. Lean back as far as possible. (At the bottom you'll be in a position to dance the limbo.) This will cause your knees to go forward, and you'll get a tremendous stretch in your thighs when you get to the bottom position. Tip: Put a two-by-four-inch board under your heels for balance and hold a plate on your chest with your free hand when you get strong enough.

Spider curls *(biceps).* Take a shoulder-width grip on a barbell and position yourself over a spider curl bench with your triceps against the flat side. Your upper arms should be perpendicular to the floor, and your torso should be parallel to the floor. Curl the bar up to your nose, pause for a count of two, lower and repeat. Alternate exercises: nonsupport dumbbell concentration curls, barbell concentration curls.

Squats *(quadricep, buttocks, lower back, hamstrings).* This exercise is a bit more dangerous than one-leg squats in the home-gym setting, but if you take the right precautions, it's one of the best movements around. Take a loaded barbell off of a rack and onto your shoulders. Back away from the rack, take a comfortable stance and squat until your thighs are just below parallel to the floor. You may want to put a two-by-four-inch board under your heels for better form and balance. Also, throughout the movement be sure to look straight ahead to prevent your lower back from rounding or arching, and keep your torso as upright as possible to maximize thigh involvement. If you're going all out on these, have a partner standing by in case you miss. Tip: Squat while straddling your exercise bench to get the right depth. This is also safer if you miss because you can sit and rest until you can get to the top to rerack the weight.

Standing calf raises *(calves).* Place a loaded barbell across your shoulders and stand on your calf block near a wall, with your feet about 12 inches apart. Lean forward and balance by placing the top of your head against the wall (a towel would be helpful here). Proceed to do calf raises, going up as high as possible and down as low as possible. Tip: You can also do these with a loaded weight belt around your waist instead of a barbell across your shoulders or on a Smith machine. Alternate exercises: one-leg calf raises, machine calf raises.

Stiff-legged deadlifts on a bench or block *(hamstrings, lower back, buttocks).* The stiff-legged deadlift really hits the lower back and hamstrings hard, not to mention the buttocks. Load a bar on your bench racks, stand up on the bench, lift the bar and take a step back. With the bar at arm's length, slowly bend at the waist, keeping the bar close to your legs as it descends. When the bar is about five inches from hitting the bench, reverse the direction and slowly pull your torso into the upright position. Tip: Placing one hand over and the other under the bar (an over-under grip) will make it more secure and keep it from slipping. Also, keep your back flat throughout the movement. Alternate exercise: The leg curl can be used as a substitute, but it doesn't work your lower back as the deadlift does.

Toes-pointed leg curls *(calves, hamstrings)*. These are done like regular leg curls, only you point your toes away from your legs, which brings the calves into play.

Undergrip bent-over barbell rows *(latissimus dorsi)*. Do these like regular bent-over barbell rows, but use an undergrip and keep your arms in close to your torso. Alternate exercises: undergrip chins, undergrip pulldowns.

Undergrip chins *(latissimus dorsi, biceps)*. Grab the chinning bar with a shoulder-width grip and your palms facing back. From a dead-hang position, pull yourself up until your clavicles touch the bar. Lower and repeat. Alternate exercises: undergrip pulldowns, undergrip bent-over rows.

Upright dumbbell rows *(deltoids)*. Take a dumbbell in each hand and stand erect. With your palms facing back, pull the dumbbells up to chest level while keeping them close to your body. Lower and repeat. Tip: Keep your hands slightly wider than shoulder width to ensure that your lateral, or side, heads get their share of the work. Alternate exercise: upright rows.

Wide-grip chins *(latissimus dorsi)*. Grip the bar about a hand width out from shoulder width on each side. Pull up, arch your lower back slightly and touch your clavicles to the bar. Tip: You can use a chair under your feet for assisted reps after you hit failure. Also, by keeping your feet on the chair throughout the set, you can more easily keep your back arched for a better lat contraction. Just don't cheat. Alternate exercise: pulldowns.

Wide-grip upright rows *(deltoids)*. Use a slightly wider-than-shoulder-width grip on these. While standing upright with the barbell hanging at arm's length, pull the bar up to your chest. Keep it close to your body. Stop at midchest level, lower slowly and repeat. If this exercise hurts your wrists or shoulders, use dumbbells for less joint restriction. Tip: Try using a lighter weight once in a while and raising the bar to your nose instead of stopping at your chest. Alternate exercise: dumbbell upright rows, dumbbell lateral raises (standing or seated).

(*Note:* For more exercise descriptions get a copy of Bill Pearl's *Keys to the Inner Universe*. This text gives a description of almost every exercise in existence and is indispensable for the beginner as well as the advanced weight trainer.)

OTHER POWER-PACKED *IRONMAN* PRODUCTS

IRONMAN BULLETIN #1: 10-WEEK SIZE SURGE
A Crash Course for Packing On Muscle Weight

This bulletin includes two high-intensity-training phases built into a 10-week cycle, the Size Surge Diet, a balanced meal-by-meal eating schedule with perfect protein, carb and fat percentages that deliver accelerated anabolic uptake and the 7 Sacred Rules for Packing On Muscle Weight You Should Never Break. One bodybuilder gained 20 pounds of muscle on this program in only 10 weeks and added 1 1/2 inches to his arms!

by Steve Holman
$9.95

IRONMAN's CRITICAL MASS
The Positions-of-Flexion Approach to Explosive Muscle Growth

Muscle fiber recruitment can triple your results, and POF is the way to achieve it. This is the original POF manual and features more than 150 dramatic photos with bodypart-by-bodypart analyses and a number of complete result-producing routines.

by Steve Holman
Photography by Michael Neveux
$19.95

COMPOUND AFTERSHOCK
POF Update 1

Move up the POF ladder of intensity with Compound Aftershock training and the Compound Aftershock routine. This book also includes the Supercompensation workout, Isolation Aftershock training and the Double-Impact technique.

by Steve Holman
$14.95

THE CRITICAL MASS VIDEO SERIES
"Critical Arms," "Critical Chest & Delts" and "Critical Legs & Back"

This is exciting live-action POF training that will truly ignite your motivation and maximize your workout effectiveness. You'll see exactly how to perform the exercises for the best size-building effects plus plenty of tips and training anylisis you can use to fire up your mass gains. See champs like Paul DeMayo blast their bodyparts into submission with this breakthrough size-building method. (You won't believe the footage of his quad training!)

$24.95 each, or all 3 for only $49.95 (you save $25)

To order by credit card call
1-800-447-0008, ext. 1

or send check or money order for the amount plus $4.50 shipping and handling to

IRONMAN Products, 1701 Ives Ave., Oxnard, CA 93033